THE I ND

OUR SECRET DESTINY

FREDERICK DODSON

COPYRIGHT

ISBN-10: 1730763944

ISBN-13: 978-1730763946

DISCLAIMER

The author is not responsible for effects readers have or allegedly have from this book, just like a driving school instructor is not responsible for his students driving. Furthermore, the information provided in this book is not a substitute for conventional medical assistance.

CONTENTS

BLUE BEINGS FROM THE PLEIADES 1

THE THREE VEILS TO TRUTH 21

QUESTION EVERYTHING 53

TYPES OF ANGELS, ENTITIES AND EXTRATERRESTRIALS.. 103

THE SECRET HISTORY OF EARTH 165

THE PLEIADES CONNECTION TO EARTH 231

HOW TO TRAVEL THE UNIVERSE 359

CHAPTER ONE

BLUE BEINGS FROM THE PLEIADES

A peculiar vision inspired the writing of this book. It was a vivid and deeply personal experience with blue-skinned aliens from the *Pleiades*. One might say it was a "lucid dream" but it wasn't — I was awake. It had a dream-like quality while being entirely real.

In my 2005 book, *Parallel Universes of Self*, I wrote about childhood encounters with blue-skinned alien beings. Neither as a child nor at the time I wrote the book, did I know *who* these beings were, what their purpose or my relation to them was. Over time, I forgot about the whole thing. A few nights before starting this book, I had my first conscious encounter with them since childhood.

Before sleep, I was in bed, eyes closed, when suddenly I felt an odd shifting motion at the center of my head, perhaps the pineal gland. It felt like a ray of light shone into the bedroom or I was transported to an alternate-reality version of my house. It was still the bedroom, but it looked like an elevated, shining version thereof. There was no fear or surprise, but a heavenly tranquility of the kind not felt in ages.

Describing higher consciousness with the vocabulary of a lower state is not that easy, unless you're a poet perhaps. Compare a gigantic palace the size of a mountain and glittering with diamonds and pearls, beside a run-down, rat-infested shack. Transpose that difference to a state of emotions instead of buildings, and you'll have an idea of what *it felt like*. Any sense of heaviness, confusion, tiredness or pressure vanishes and you are filled with a crystal clarity and wonderous rapture. There is a sense of accelerated intelligence and depth perception. And that was just *one* level higher (or on the 1 to 1000 scale in my book, *Levels of Energy*, 100 levels higher).

My thought quality was augmented to a level of brilliance I had forgotten even existed. You know all these brain-boosting pills and brain gym books they offer up in stores? They make promises of the abilities I was experiencing in this "dream", but never deliver. You know this endless guru gibberish about raising your consciousness after many decades of training? I had elevated to that within seconds. Soon my thoughts revolved around pleasant scenarios and memories of Earth life, all surrounded by glistening, lustrous, intense light and brand new ways of making sense of various events.

One particular image was a memory of me walking on a boardwalk, surrounded by seagulls. I felt strangely uplifted on that day, inspired from within. It was shown that on that day I was surrounded by some light from above. This light was oscillating in different colors as if it were a piano, spread over the boardwalk, myself and the seagulls. There were other memories, and I don't know why they were shown to me. It was as if they were saying, "Look, these were your encounters with the spiritual realm in the last several years." **Depending on consciousness level, we not only remember other things, we remember them differently.**

I had entered a higher consciousness influenced by some external presence in the room. **My awareness was high enough to recognize the presence and its intentions and its history instantly.** Nothing was mysterious or foggy. It was neither waking, sleeping or dreaming, but a *category of its own* — a vision, perhaps. It was as if a communication portal between my bedroom and a star system far away had been opened.

Then I let go as if letting the body fall asleep while my mind seemed to be receiving a transmission of sorts. It was understood that, in order to perceive more thoroughly. I'd have to let the body sleep. There was a clear perception of something *transmitting* information into my skull from a source hovering in the sky above my house. Because it was deeply pleasant, full of warm, tingling, swirling sensations, I welcomed it rather than snapping myself awake. Imagine the polar opposite of a nightmare. I looked up an antonym to "nightmare" but didn't find any. Why isn't this type of experience encoded in our language?

The Blue Beings that I had frequent encounters with in childhood, gently reappeared in my field of vision. This time I saw they were clearly humanoid. At first, they stayed vaguely at the periphery of my field of inner vision, as if in some kind of cosmic etiquette, but eventually eased to its forefront. Accompanying their presence was this realization: While for me, thirty-five years had passed since I last saw them, for them it was only a few years. Their time passed differently. The higher the level, the less time passes so that to exceedingly high realms one second might be a million years to us.

I used an online tool to make this image of what they looked like:

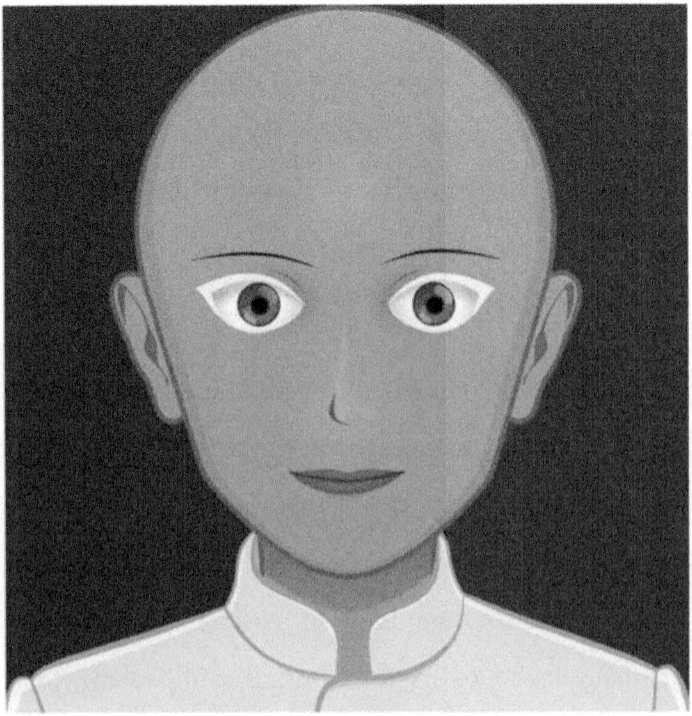

They were floating in mid-air, wearing uniforms of an alien texture that was both lighter than any material we have on Earth, yet more durable. I knew that no bullet could penetrate it. Through their energy-level, many things were clear to me in their presence that had not been clear to me outside of it. The main difference with humans is that their eyes are bigger, their irises and pupils more pronounced and all of them have peaceful facial expressions. They looked like people who don't experience any strife (yet were aware of others' struggles).

Among other things, some of the contents of this book were telepathically transmitted to me. In my normal, everyday mindset, these ideas would seem like nonsense, pulp fiction even. But in this presence, it all made *perfect sense.* I was reminded of the very important fact that some beings can have a significant influence on what we feel, think, know or fail to know. Even now, after the event I sometimes wonder about this book I am writing: *Am I really writing this? This stuff could be construed as the rantings of a madman. What about my reputation as a success-coach? What kind of success-coach writes about visitations by aliens and out of body travels? How am I supposed to communicate any of this publicly?*

You see, I began writing this right after the event, but three months later, I am doing an edit of the book and am back in my normal, everyday life state and wondering about this book's contents. Fortunately for the reader, at this point in my life, I care more about experiential truth than reputation. How are we ever going to evolve if everyone keeps their most interesting experiences to themselves? Rather than trying to fit this material into Earth's prevailing paradigms, I'll simply share what I perceived.

What happened next, I did not foresee at all. They showed me an old scene from my life, when I was around the age of twenty-seven. I was told that it was *they* who had set up the *incident* on that day, for their own purposes. At the time I did not have the slightest inkling that the event was something other than it appeared to be. Imagine the surprise to find out that something that looks *mundane*, worth forgetting even, is something entirely different than you thought it was. That's the most typical and fun part of higher states — events being *reframed* to something other than what they were before.

At the age of twenty-seven, I was living alone in an apartment on the outskirts of the city of Munich, Germany. My doorbell rang and two police officers (or what I thought were police officers!) stood at the door.

They told me that they were investigating a murder and needed to see whether I owned a pair of white Nike sneakers. I did indeed. I asked them how they knew. They told me that the murderer was wearing white Nike sneakers and that they had gone to local sports gear shops to find the names of every single person who had bought those particular shoes. I found nothing odd about it at the time, but now, in retrospect, it does seem a little contrived. Once they confirmed that I owned a pair of those sneakers, they asked whether they could take a sample of my blood for DNA testing. Respectful of the weight of their job, I consented to the blood sample without hesitation. And again, in retrospect it does seem strange: Complete strangers show up at my door asking for a blood sample. Without even taking a closer look at their officer badges, I let them poke a needle into my finger and extract blood. If the same happened today, I'd probably ask a few more questions. I guess we grow more circumspect with age. After taking the sample, they left and I never heard from them or about the case again.

I recall looking into the newspapers about the murder on the same day, and the days thereafter, but I found *nothing* on it. I also recall vaguely wondering whether there was more to the visit than met the eye, but I never followed up on it. The silent voice of intuition was, as it was so many times, ignored. That's the thing with underdeveloped intuition: There is a vague sense of there being more than meets the eye, but it's so vague we can't make sense of it and simply move on as if all were normal. It is amazing how much we actually know without *admitting* to ourselves that we already know it, pretending we have to go out and look for the answers. Our society really has been set up in a way to keep certain types of knowledge under wraps.

The Blue Beings identified themselves as originating in the star-system of the *Pleiades*. This took me by surprise as I could never quite peg down their origin. I knew virtually nothing about the Pleiades except that they were a cluster of stars. In fact, I had spent a lifetime *ignoring* all those books and New Age movies about "aliens from the Pleiades".

Did I start reading up on it after this event? You bet. But what I got from all that New Age Pleiadean literature didn't "vibe" with my freshly-gained understanding. Some of the material seemed loosely related to what I had experienced, but much of it felt made up. So I had to, once again, write my own book on it. That's the story of my life — looking for books to help me understand my experiences, but not finding the right books and therefore, writing my own.

While showing me the long-gone scene from my life, with two police officers dressed in casual clothing, they telepathically explained, that it was *they* who had wanted my DNA. Yes, it was they who, through contacts on Earth, had arranged for the "police" to visit me.

I was calm enough to inquire why they wanted it. In the childhood encounters, I was too overwhelmed and blissful to ever ask questions. But at my more mature age of forty-four, I was determined to get some of the answers that had evaded me half a lifetime. For earthly sentiments, their answer was truly bizarre, almost laughable: They said they had *purchased the right* to get a sample of my blood. They showed me that they were using my DNA and that of thousands of other Earthlings to seed and populate distant planets throughout the Universe. In my heightened state, this did not at all seem strange to me. While writing this I am back to normal and it actually sounds funny. If true, there is a cloned version of me somewhere on another planet!

No wonder I spent half of my life researching "other versions of self". I was *shown* the other "me": He was living a life in an utterly foreign environment, millions of lightyears far away. He did look better than me, as if he were not subject to the "wear and tear" of life on Earth. He was surrounded by rolling green hills on the outskirts of a village of sorts. What I remember from the village is that its houses were made of a kind of flexible glass that could would very slowly shift in color, somehow depending on the outer light conditions. There were things that I saw on that planet that I didn't understand, just like an infant wouldn't understand what a laptop is.

And while the general tone of that environment was higher, I sensed that it was not without problems.

A common misconception is that advanced civilizations are all without issues and everyone spends all day playing the harp on a cloud. There are problem-free realms up there, but all planets in the physical universe have duality and contrast, and where there is contrast, there are problems. Their crime rate is much lower than on Earth, but the concept of crime still exists. In fact, these Pleiadeans are themselves involved in intergalactic warfare. It took me only a split second to realize this, due to my heightened state. Rather than deifying them as "beings of light", I not only saw how they are more advanced than us, but also the downsides of their society.

It seemed that my consciousness level had been elevated to be equal to that of the Pleiadeans. I was no longer all that starry-eyed about the encounter itself but rather glad at the super-lucid state I found myself in. It was like I had taken a smart-pill. If any human were able to retain this level of intelligence in daily life, their lives would be rather easy to handle. I recall wondering whether we have stuff put in our food, drink, toothpaste or air to turn us into morons. So radically light, fun and smart was the mind-state that it put the entirety of "life on Earth" in question.

This version of me seemed younger than me. His skin was softer and his hair fuller. He was holding a kind of electronic notebook, but I didn't know its purpose. His profession had something to do with those green rolling hills I saw him closely inspecting. There were no trees in that area, only endless round hills. Maybe he was a landscaper or land buyer, I didn't know. But then I *did* know. In this state, you look at something for a moment, then you understand it. His job was to survey land for where to build various structures. And once I knew that, I also knew that this wasn't the right land for what he was looking for and that he hadn't come to that realization yet. And then I knew that it wasn't the right land because the soil was too soft. And then I knew that the soil was too soft because of special rain conditions in the area. And then I realized that this entire part of the planet had these soil issues and that he was actually tasked with solving the entire issue. If he couldn't find locations to build, he would have to find ways to change the soil. I also realized that if I didn't deliberately interrupt this thought process, ever deeper levels of understanding would just keep piling up, connecting, extrapolating, concluding. I marveled at what the mind is capable of when accompanied by higher energy.

Looking at him was an odd sensation, because I knew a number of things about him, merely based on shared DNA. It proved to me that DNA does go a long way in shaping us. I knew he was a peaceful person but would get nervous if he couldn't pursue a purpose. I also knew that he had to discipline himself a little more than others in order to maintain an athletic body shape. These things appeared to be exactly the same with him. Something else very odd that I learned was that while he had an individual soul that *differed* from mine, his soul had to come from the same *Oversoul* as mine. I didn't know whether I believed in the Oversoul concept or not, until this event. It was now *clear* to me: This sort of body could only "carry" a certain type of soul. **The soul and body have to be compatible.** The Oversoul can be imagined as a sort of central energy from which many other souls spread out. Imagine your hand as the Oversoul and the fingers as the individual souls. So while we were not the same finger, we were the same hand. Put differently, I recognized how we were *similar* and how we were *different.* He was like me but he was not me. That was a unique feeling that I had never experienced in my waking life on Earth.

I was puzzled about how the Blue Beings came to have a "purchase right" on a sample of my blood. Do I not own my body? I asked them about this. Then they referred me to teachings I myself have published on the principle of "non-intervention by extraterrestrials". They were not allowed to intervene or interact directly with humans. They were not allowed to visit, but somehow it was legal for them to purchase a few genetic samples if they paid for it. They did not directly tell me who they paid, who "owned" Planet Earth or which planet was being seeded with my DNA, but I actually picked up on it at a sub-telepathic level.

Above a certain point, elevated intelligence becomes indiscernible from supernatural ability. Instead, the Blue Beings made it clear that they were *obliged* to tell me what they were doing or that it was illegal to extract my blood without the consent of my own "Higher Self" and without telling me. That puzzled me even more: So they do not need my conscious consent beforehand, they only need the consent of my "Higher Self"? But after it's done, they also have to tell my conscious self?

The more I learn, the less I seem to know. The Blue Beings visit to me, after thirty-five years, was to "wrap things up" and bring closure to the whole affair. They left by fading out of my awareness, and I fell into deep sleep only to awaken to birds chirping in the morning.

I began writing this book two days after the event and I am still amused by it. Something I considered to *be the most mystical and deep experiences of my life* was nothing more than a mundane *purchase transaction* of an alien race! Their visiting me in childhood was to "check me out" for the quality of my DNA. Then, decades later (for them probably just months later), they sent in two fake "cops" to extract my blood. Another decade and a half later, they tell me what happened and that the deal is wrapped up and another version (or perhaps several) of me exist on other planets.

I have described these childhood encounters in books, videos and seminars. Many people have asked me about them with glowing eyes. They seemed profound beyond words. But to these aliens, they were just going on a shopping tour and I was just a sample on that tour.

It is our comparatively low state that makes things that are mundane to them, mysterious and amazing to us. While writing these words I notice a cat staring at me through a window. She looks at me with stunned fascination, as if mystified at what I am doing. But to me, it's just writing on a laptop.

At least it does seem like I got something in return for my blood sample. I got some of their energy and their knowledge. And just a little bit of that has spawned an entire career on Planet Earth.

CHAPTER TWO

THE THREE VEILS TO TRUTH

This book contains what I know about angels, aliens and entities in relation to humanity, the hidden history of Planet Earth and a possible New Enlightened Earth. It is a one-of-a-kind read because I draw partially from personal experience, partially from consciousness research and lucid dreaming as well as cross-referencing with what we know from science, metaphysics, religion and mythology. Thus, a clear picture of our overall situation emerges.

Truth is one of my highest values, even above safety. But as there is no such thing as perfection in this realm, parts of it may be unintentionally flawed. I ask you to use discernment when reading. You have "the three I's" to help you with that: intuition, intelligence and the internet. Use them to do your own research rather than just relying on what I or others say.

It's not an easy task to write a book about something that is entirely clear to me but sounds so outlandish to a normal mindset. Do I actually have to try and prove what I'm saying here? I don't mean to sound smug, but imagine living in the U.S. and having to prove to someone that China and the Chinese exist. To you it's obvious, you have been to China, spent time with its people and do not feel the need to prove that fact. However, when you tell the tale, people will say, "That sounds fantastical. Got any proof?"

It seems cumbersome to have to elaborate. I'd say, "Why not just travel to China and go see for yourself?" I am not in a court, nor do I have any desire to prove something. My intention here is to share my travel report, nothing more, nothing less. And until you have seen it for yourself, feel free to view this book as science fiction. In fact, it would feel tedious to me to have to try to prove this, just like you would feel bored to have to prove the existence of China.

I do, however, believe that at a certain level of consciousness, these materials are obvious. While a few details here and there may be off, you can grasp the overall nature of these realities intuitively. It's truth can also be understood by its logical consistency and alignment with everything else we know. What's more, I can and will give you instructions on how to obtain some of this knowledge through direct experience of your own.

Something important I've discovered: If you know yourself well, you'll know reality and the nature of the Universe well. If you are honest with yourself and others, you will see more truth. It is your own integrity that reveals all the mysteries of life to you.

This book is vastly different from my previous books, especially those I have written in on success coaching. You might dismiss it, but that's alright with me because I do not think it is of utmost importance to believe in any of this. I do, however, think it is important to believe in your own inherent power to live an abundant and happy life. Whether you believe in aliens or not, is of no concern to me. I write this out of the enjoyment of arcane information, not to persuade. I write it foremost *to make sense of various encounters* I have had in my own life. Nor do I mind skepticism; it is a sign of intelligence. In fact, my own skepticism of official versions of reality, as taught in schools, is what made writings such as this possible.

I believe that we experience the karmic consequences for the information we put out into the world. If I put false information out, I will get false information back. I therefore believe that lies, shoddy research, exaggeration and delusion would hurt myself the most. The more people I expose to falsehood, the more negative consequences I create for myself. It is from this belief that I do my very best to report with accuracy. But I wholeheartedly believe that what is contained in this book will age well in the next few hundred years as we allow for more about ourselves to be revealed.

The expected result of reading this book is so that you may understand your place in the broader Universe, gain the skills to communicate with that broader Universe and open up a pathway to becoming a *cosmic citizen.* Human beings are not as close to higher cosmic consciousness as we fancy ourselves to be. The truth that many of the books out there on "alien ontact" that you find in the New Age and UFOs sections, skim over or fail to mention entirely, is that most extraterrestrial and extra-dimensional beings are not all that interested in humanity, in the same way that many of us not all that interested in animals. To understand life more clearly, release your Earth-centric view and adopt a galaxy-wide view.

On the bright side, we are very much loved and protected by our Creator as well higher beings that understand our purpose and if we take responsibility for raising our consciousness and energy, we can one day join an *already thriving* galactic community. This galaxy has been thriving with life and spacefaring civilizations long before humans came on the scene and will still be thriving long after humans disappear. Likewise, humanity was hustling and bustling long before you were born and will continue to long after you disappear, if you look at it from a non-self-centered viewpoint.

The Universe existed before this galaxy did and will still exist after this galaxy fades away. Everything is coming and going, so the story I will tell here, as fantastical or crazy as it may sound, is really only a small part of a much larger context.

The first person who read this manuscript said "*Wow, that's really, really far out. Are you sure you want to publish that?*" But to me, it's not really that far out. I'm only describing events that happened in one of the small villages of the Universe (Planet Earth), but these are of little consequence to the whole country (galaxy) or even world (Universe). *"So why write it if it's of no consequence?"* you might ask. Because you, the reader, resonating with a higher frequency, is of real consequence in the grand scheme of things. In previous books, I have attempted to provide the techniques and methods to raise your consciousness. This book attempts another path: I am providing you with the knowledge a person on Earth's next level of consciousness has, as if Planet Earth were *already* on that level.

I have asked myself why it is that things that seem obvious to me, appear offbeat to others. The answer is, that either I am *delusional* or I am allowing myself to see things that are not visible to many others. If you've read a few of my books and followed my real-life experiences, you may understand why I do not give much credence to what is considered "knowledge" in most circles. This is because my life works beautifully. I am blessed with abundant health, wealth, family and friends. Some might say that my life working well does not prove that I am not insane, but I use *well-being* as a measure of success and success as a measure of alignment-with-truth.

There appears to be an organized effort to hide and confuse human nature and reality so that it requires a detective-like penchant for puzzle-solving, to uncover ontological Truth. In our society, there are three main paradigms that we look at to gain truth: Science, Religion "Alternative" ideas.

While all three provide tidbits of truth, to stay relevant, they also serve as *veils* to higher truth. I call science, religion and "alternative" views *The Three Veils to Truth* because they cloak, mask, cover a higher reality.

If these veils were not firmly ingrained in our minds, we'd be free and already part of a galactic society of peace and prosperity. Free energy, interstellar travel, teleportation, instant healing and possibly even time travel would not be mocked as "impossible" but considered normal, or at least worthy of research.

The problem with that is that then Planet Earth would no longer be a place where souls come to balance out negative karma. It would no longer be a place of harvesting a select few every couple of thousand years. So **there is a positive purpose to hiding the greater truths from us, one of them being: It is our task, as individuals, to regain them.**

What? Did this author just say humans are harvested? Yes, he did. And if you look at the big picture, it doesn't sound all that crazy. Charles Darwin tells of a process of "natural selection" and "survival of the fittest". Religions tell us that only the pure reach Heaven. Can you see how both of these stories essentially refer to a process of *selection*?

I recently learned that my own DNA had been harvested to seed other planets. That seems to be one of the aspects of the overall game here. Earth appears to be a place where humans grow like fruits and are then harvested — not in the sense of being eaten by some alien force — but in the sense of being put in the places they belong.

There is a theory that humans are nothing but food for another species and that we are being allowed to multiply so that these vampires have enough food stock. Fortunately, as interesting as it sounds, I haven't seen anything to suggest that. Were I to buy into that it would create a no-hope situation and mass suicides. What appears to be happening instead is that Planet Earth was created for souls to grow in certain unique conditions. Just like you would plant grapes in certain favorable conditions to produce great wine. Souls that aren't yet ready, are re-planted here. That's called reincarnation.

Souls that are ready, ascend and fulfill another purpose at a higher level. That's called ascension.

Almost everyone reading this, is going to ascend. If you are reading this, it means you are mature enough to lift some of these veils. In my view, it means you have done well enough to have *attracted* this type of information. In fact, almost anyone who reads these types of books share character traits that give them immunity toward Earth-centric, negative brainwashing.

You have come to realize that what is called "science" is partially not science but rather a belief system that might be called materialistic atheism. What is called "religion" is partially not religion but cultic absolutism. And parts of the "alternative spirituality" are not actually new but unrefined astral-level (rather than spiritual-level) teaching. You have the guts to realize that all three main "paths of knowledge" contain a lot of gibberish. Only very few people acknowledge that. And most people are so overwhelmed with work and entertainment that their attention span doesn't even allow for a review of these basic paths, much less those that go beyond. That is my job. I do have the time, interest and attention to research and leave no stone unturned.

An example regarding extraterrestrials:

A religious fanatic will tell you there is no such thing as extraterrestrials. "God only created humans. All aliens are demons. All angels are demons in disguise!" I have entertained this idea and found it to be false.

A scientific materialist will tell you there is no such thing as extraterrestrials. "It took an unlikely chain of coincidences for humans to exist. That's unlikely to have happened anywhere else in the Universe. There is no evidence for aliens. Angels and demons? No such thing. fairy tales." This is not science. I call it *Scientism.* It is a cult, no different than a dogmatic religious belief system.

In a closed mentality, science and religion, the "twin pillars of civilization" only allow for a very limited amount of knowledge, spawning a limited amount of civilization. Sure, they have helped us achieve a lot, but we could achieve *so much more* if the veils were lifted.

Unsatisfied by this obvious nonsense about us being "alone" in the Universe, you'll consult "alternative sources" and come across New Age books, occult books, alternative science books, etc. But you'll find plenty of flaws there too. As if those "grey aliens" who show up in the most creepy manner at night, scaring the living daylights out of you, and inserting "anal probes" into your body without your consent are "beings of higher consciousness and intelligence that are here to save us."

The weakness of these "alternative" teachings is that they mistake beings of the astral realm with extraterrestrial beings or those of the spiritual realms. That's why *discerning between astral, spiritual and extraterrestrial* is one of the points of this book.

I have always seen it as my task to break through the three veils or to merge them when possible. Have the veils been put in place intentionally? Is there a vast conspiracy to keep the truth hidden from us? Or is it through our own limited view that we are blind? The answer is both. There are people and beings that do not want us to awaken. Why? Because the purpose of this planet is for lower consciousness beings to find ways to ascend. Hence, they want to keep it lower consciousness. Otherwise, lost souls have no place to go to cleanse themselves. But even so, as individuals, we have the power to awaken to higher realities by our own free will. Even if this planet stays unenlightened, the individual can achieve enlightenment. Even if there were an agenda to keep us enslaved, it's our own responsibility to rise above and break free. What I know for sure is that each one of us has the inherent power to liberate ourselves. Ultimately then, we are ignorant by *choice*.

While ignorance is not bliss, it's certainly comfortable. I could easily live the rest of my in my little bubble, on my little property, minding my own business instead of putting myself out there to teach this stuff. And that would be fine. But it wouldn't help my own ascension or that of humanity.

It is good to have a dose of critical thinking, but the "skepticism" of the *scientism* sort, is not *genuinely skeptical* because it is only skeptical of one thing: Paranormal and spiritual experience. It is not skeptical of itself, nor any other paradigm out there. That's not skepticism, it's cultism. Hence *scientism.* You know scientism very well. These-are the folks that claim that consciousness research is a "pseudoscience", that ancient alien research is a "pseudoscience", that reiki is a "pseudoscience" that chakras are a "pseudoscience" and that "love is nothing more than a chemical reaction". According to them, the only thing "real" are the things they can measure with their limited tools.

Nor is the so-called "scientific method" the tell-all, end-all. I can see the Pleiadean experience mentioned above from a skeptical viewpoint: Perhaps it's just a dream I had, with no bearing on reality, just a fantasy and now I am writing a book of fiction based upon it. The reason I do not believe in what scientism says, is because trusting in their evaluations has proven a mistake many times in my life. Had I followed their rubbish "advice", I would not be healthy, wealthy, successful and happy as I am these days. It's really as simple as that.

Another explanation, this one a bit more paranoid: Maybe some sinister agency used psychotronic devices to beam and implant this information into my mind. They want me to write this book to mislead people for their own nefarious agenda. I bring this up, because I know I have discerning readers who consider any possibility. The reason I doubt this explanation though, is because many good things have been happening to me before and after the experience. Good things happening is a sign of being under a good influence. Bad things happening is a sign of being under a bad influence. Make sense? As a child, my parents took me to church and I heard plenty of pastors espouse the following paranoid view:

"Demons always appear as beings of light. Demons do not appear as monsters. They bring with them peace and bliss."

While this type of deception is certainly possible, and crooked people and beings certainly can pose as "the good guys", it is not only false but outright dangerous to believe that good things are universally tools of deception. Some people turn teachings like this into the idea that every time someone mentions peace and bliss, they are dealing with evil. How unwholesome is that?

Using discernment, again, the truth is more something like this: There are negative people and negative beings who pose as good beings. Imagine a criminal putting on a fancy suit to appear respectable. However, if you are at peace inside, you will always intuit deception. Or you will see signs of it. Negativity cannot mask as positivity for too long. Unless you are at a very low level of consciousness, you'll be able to tell a "bad guy" from a "good guy" a mile away. You'll smell it. The same applies to non-physical beings. If there is a "demon" appearing as a "being of light", as paranoid Christians say, then the deception will be seen very soon or a little later, by the *fruits* it bears. Eventually it will have to reveal itself. A negative source would not keep delivering positive results over weeks, months, years and decades. That would be self-defeating to its negative intent. And that's why the idea that positive equals negative doesn't make any sense.

Yes, deception does exist, but genuinely positive people and beings also exist. And it's not all that difficult to discern between the two. You know that you are aligned with what is good, true and beautiful, if your life is healthy, moderately wealthy and happy. So no, I do not believe some evil agency has been implanting false information into me to get me to write books. Because that would mean I am a delusional puppet. And if I were a delusional puppet, I wouldn't feel as enriched and healthy as I am.

There are several other possible explanations for my Pleiadean experience. Considering them is true open mindedness and critical inquiry — a trait lacking in many New Age and "alternative science" authors. But proponents of the atheistic-materialistic *scientism* kind go the other extreme, overusing skepticism to the point of not arriving at *any* usable data. The final aim of their "inquiry" is always the "debunking" of any extraordinary claim, so that when they are done, there is nothing at all unusual, mysterious, amazing or interesting about life. If someone sets out to debunk a claim of the paranormal, they will end up with that result because any other result would create cognitive dissonance. To get a feel for how this cult thinks and operates, you can visit online sites such as "The Skeptics Dictionary" or "Rational Wiki". But this cult is not limited to these designated areas. They also have a firm grip on the editing of Wikipedia, Google and mass media outlets, filing yearly lawsuits and information removal requests in their zealous drive for their version of "truth". Any researcher who would look into who exactly finances this *multi-billion dollar information war*, might be surprised by what they find. Any alternative-info author who writes books such as these, has had encounters with *them.*

I've seen dozens of genuine spiritual and extraterrestrial authors mocked, derided and their characters assassinated. One of the activist "skeptics" misgivings is that these authors "make money off the gullible". Are they envious of success? Do they not trust that people can form their own thoughts and views? I don't know. But I am certain that it is not I or my readers that are gullible. Gullible are those who do not question reality and take everything said by the "authorities on education" at face value. Gullible is to assume that life on Earth is a coincidence and there is "nothing to see out there". Such beliefs shut down any sort of curiosity or desire to investigate. I'd say that curiosity and research are the foundation of learning and expanding.

I believe the Pleiadean event was not merely a dream but a genuine encounter with real extraterrestrials because of the intensity of the experience. Decades of research have taught me that deceptive intent (be it through humans or aliens) never comes with lasting positive states of emotion. If positive emotions are involved, they are fleeting and vague. One could say that "by states of consciousness you shall know them". The experience left no wounds, no blisters, no scars, no trauma, no worry, no bad health, no sudden change of behavior. Instead, it left a sense of purpose, belonging, freedom and wellness that echoed for weeks thereafter.

Religious and spiritual types are certainly better at accepting the "extraordinary", but even here we find areas of strange narrow-mindedness. No doubt some of this is by design, but it's also partially because higher-level information that comes to us is filtered through Earth's relatively dense energy level. In other words, the original messages of a Buddha, Jesus, Mohammed, Krishna are pristine, but become sullied and distorted the longer they circulate on Earth.

As I now understand, books like the one you are reading right now, shouldn't even be written without a prior higher level of energy. All *valid* information is gained in *higher states* and must then be translated into human words after one "comes back down to Earth". I know readers who prefer the books that I wrote in mundane, non-enlightened states. They'll says, "I loved your book, *Prosperity Consciousness*, it's the best! But I don't know about your book "*Journeys in Spectral Consciousness*, it's kind of weird. Well, that book was written in the highest consciousness and it's my least best-selling book, whereas the former was written in a "normal" state of consciousness and it's my best-selling one. So number of sales, positive reviews and "likes" on the internet, don't really tell me anything about the *quality* of a book, they merely tell me about Earth's level of consciousness. Sure, the bestselling books are more practical, that's why they sell so well. But they are not the "best" in a spiritual sense.

After the experience with the Blue Beings, I began reading everything I could about the Pleiades and Pleiadeans. As you might have guessed, contemporary *scientism* offered *nothing* on Pleiadeans. That's amazing to me. Here is an entire culture of extraterrestrial beings and what we consider science has no books, no articles, no teachings about them. What kind of "science" is that? Fortunately, there are *millions* of open-minded scientists out there. I know that, because they send me feedback about my books. But they have been restrained from speaking out due to the cult of *scientism* which has infiltrated universities and the mass media.

I once wrote an entire book about this cult — how they operate, how they are funded, what argumentation methods they use to suppress free thought. But finally, I deleted the entire book. Why bother? I'd only attract lawsuits and smear articles in the press.

Fact is, that most people are already clued into their vibe and have rejected it. The majority of scientists are actually open-minded about anything. And many of the religious scholars I have talked to are also open-minded about anything. The reason for this is that Earth's level of consciousness has undergone quite a shift in the last few decades. Things I wouldn't dare have talked about only twenty years ago, are now mundane conversation among both the educated and the uneducated. Hardly anyone has difficulty discussing aliens, entities, other dimensions, time-travel or any other "paranormal" subject out there. This is mainly thanks to the internet. The internet has taught people that "regular folks" *think about this kind of stuff casually and regularly.* I deleted my book because its outdated. We have already improved significantly and there is no need to beat a dying horse.

Not finding any scientific books on Pleiadeans, I went to see what religions say about them. And again, the information was *scarce*. There is some, but its *cryptic* to the point of being useless for the general populace. I'll show those references in this book.

Last but not least, I had to resort to the literature of New Age spirituality, which fortunately does have *a whole lot to say* on Pleiadeans. Unfortunately, many (not all) New-Agers lack discernment between the astral and the spiritual. Among these there are also shortcomings in critical thinking. Some of the material I found online was so incoherent, it made me laugh out loud and even feel a little embarrassed for writing a book that so prominently features Pleiadeans. After this book comes out, I am going to be listed in the same category as some of these nut jobs. Some of what I found, however, is good and added to the research in this book.

To provide an example of how the two veils of scientific-skepticism and New Age kooks work together as two polar opposites to muddy the waters, allow me to quote a section from the *scientism* website "Rational Wiki" on the Pleiadeans:

Pleiadeans, also known as elves Nordic aliens or Plejaren are humanoid aliens that come from the stellar systems surrounding the Pleiades stars, and they're really, really, really concerned about Earth and our future. (Since the Pleiades are a pretty group of stars and since they're even more beautiful through telescopes, anything connected with them has to be good and kind, right?) So concerned are they, they've contacted[1] certain[2] special[3] people[4] to[5] channel[6] them[7] and[8] convey their message. Which isn't always consistent. The Pleiadeans either came from a group called the Lyrans[4], or coexisted with the Lyrans,[3] or the distinctions between Lyran, Pleiadean, and Sirians don't really exist.[3] Native Americans are of Pleiadean descent,[2] or white people are of Lyran descent,[4] or humans are of no notable relation to either.[3] They can either switch between the third and the ninth dimension,[9] or they exist solely in the fifth dimension[4] (which is apparently made of love and creativity), or just live in non-specific dimensions higher than three.[6] Basically, the only things generally agreed upon by the Pleiadeans themselves is that they want to help Earth and let humanity ascend to higher dimensions.

Source: https://rationalwiki.org/wiki/Pleiadians

Can you see the problem here? First New Agers set up completely made-up stories with no basis in experience, inconsistent with anything else and easily refutable and worth mocking. Then skeptics come in and mock and debunk the whole thing. The formula is so easy, yet it is used over and over again:

1. Take a truth you would like to cover-up and publish nonsense around it.

2. Then dismiss the *entire* subject by debunking these falsehoods.

The same article does mention just one true fact, but it's unlikely to be recognized as such because it's buried among so much nonsense. See if you can spot it:

Pleiadeans are somehow connected to Atlantis[3] and Lemuria.[4] Reiki, ear candling, Shiatsu, reflexology, aromatherapy, and crystal healing all came from the

Pleiadeans[6]. The Pleiadeans brought dolphins to Earth – we know so because JFK's spirit has contacted a human through automatic writing to tell us so.[14] Jesus was a Pleiadean, as was his father,[4] though his mother was Lyran. They love sex[9] (the Pleiadeans do, not Jesus and his family… though they must too if they're Pleiadeans). The Pleiadeans are helping us fight the evil space reptiles[8] (and you thought we couldn't connect this to Reptoids) as part of the battle against the Illuminati. They are Old, Old, Old Earth creationists, and think Earth is 626 billion years old.[4]

There is only one factual statement in the entire paragraph. The rest is nonsense to a greater extent. "JFKs spirit has contacted us to tell us so" is an example of nonsense to a greater extent. "Jesus was a Pleiadean" is also nonsense, but to a lesser extent because the Christian agenda is in alignment with that of the Pleiadeans, as we will see later.

So which of the statements is true? Or which of these statements do I claim is true? No, it's not the first statement. Pleiadeans are not directly connected to Atlantis and Lemuria.

It's "Pleiadeans are helping us fight evil space reptiles". I consider that to be the only true statement. But the way it is phrased, makes it look like *the silliest* of all statements.

In its core, *this book is about the wars of the ancient extraterrestrial and interdimensional serpent against the extraterrestrial but humanoid Pleiadeans and the interdimensional blue Pleiadeans.* As preposterous as that may sound right now, it's actually fairly easy to see. In fact, almost every religion and piece of cultural mythology tells us of this specific war, albeit in a veiled way. The upcoming chapters will go into detail on this war.

But if that is true, you would never learn it from paragraphs such as the one above. Whether you research the topic with the "skeptics" or with the New Agers or even "conspiracy theorists", you'd only be left confused in the end and give up the search. By the time any sane and intelligent person gets done reading either the skeptic's side or the believer's side, he will be thoroughly *turned off* of the topic. You see, there is a reason why we hardly know anything about anything in regard to the populated cosmos.

An awareness of The Three Veils to Truth has kept me from writing about extraterrestrials for a long time, even though I have always known a great deal about them. The misinformation on the subject is such, that anything I might add to the topic could easily be dismissed as just more madness. It would be like introducing a piece of diamond to a swamp. The diamond would just get swallowed up.

With all the nonsense published on this topic, who is to say that my writings aren't just more of the same? Well, you'll just have to take my word for it that not *all* things written on this are nonsense. In fact, any topic that is full of confusion and argument and noisy online fights, is likely to have a *core* of truth to it that is meant to covered-up by that noise. The truth of the matter is usually found when one calms the mind, lets go of extremes and seeks out open-minded but rational, non-agenda-driven, non-marketing-driven, non-sensationalist and good-willed sources of information. Fortunately, there are a lot of good people out there who research for the sake of research.

The only way to break through the veil (which is an anagram of "evil"), is to reject the artificial division of these paradigms and to focus on truth for truth's sake with all your heart.

CHAPTER THREE

QUESTION EVERYTHING

After the Pleiadean event, I questioned the events of my life more deeply. Just one high-energy event can lead an to an entirely different lifepath. I tread the fine line between synchronicity-awareness and paranoia. Knowing that "nothing is as it seems" allows us to see a deeper *interconnectedness* of everything. If this keener awareness is mixed with fear, it can turn sour and is then called paranoia. Without the fear, its merely awareness.

Synchronicity of Sevens

The visitation from the Pleiades, which are also known as the *Seven Sisters*, occurred just one week after moving into a new house. Relocation is a reflection of a change of consciousness. You change inside, things change outside. The address number of the new house adds up to the number seven. Up to that point, all the house addresses I have lived were number five or added up to five — yes, *all of them*, and we are talking about a dozen different addresses. For the first time in my life, it added up to seven, revealing that I had now entered a new flow or timeline.

Mentioning this to my wife, she raised her eyebrows and said "I had a dream!" She told me she saw the doorway of our new house and a bright and shining number "7" right above it. She didn't know what it meant at the time. In fact, she had the dream while we were still looking for houses and said the dream reassured her we'd find just the right one for us.

After moving in, I noticed that, above the entrance, there was an etching of a sun with seven rays. I had noticed the etching before purchasing the house, but I only noticed the seven rays afterward.

The house itself is near the top of a hill and the area as a whole is known to have seven hills. So, the house number adding up to seven, the etching of seven rays, surrounded by seven hills and preceded by my wife's dream of the house being associated with the number seven. What are the odds of that? Apparently, it had been necessary for me to move to this place of sevens before being again visited by the beings from the Seven Stars.

As the weeks passed, I recalled other strange episodes of my life. If those police officers were not who they said they were, then who else was not who they seemed to be? What other events were filtered through a veil of smug unawareness?

Implants of Unknown Origin

Every time I pass through Tel Aviv airport, their security scanner detects a *metal object in my right leg*. I have passed or landed there about five times throughout my life, and *every single time* I am strip-searched, questioned by several agents and my leg is examined as if it were a bomb. I am then detained for about forty minutes while I watch other passengers pass by without problems. This is the only airport where I experience this scenario every single time.

I didn't know that there appeared to be something in my leg until my last visit. Being non-paranoid, I *always assume the best*, so I thought that this airport just has stricter measures than others. I convinced myself that I felt much safer with their over-the-top strict measures.

But the last time it happened, I *finally* questioned it. I had the audacity to go behind a booth that contained the scanners and take a look. I saw the right leg lighting up. The officer, who had gone away for a moment (they always go away for a moment when they see my scan results) reappeared with other officers and told me that I was not allowed to enter the area. He gently removed me from there.

I asked him why my right leg was lighting up. Suddenly, I was surrounded by five officers staring at me quizzically.

He said, "Maybe you have a medical device there. That's what is causing the alert. We just have to make sure it's safe."

In all these years they had never shared that bit of information with me. They only shared it after I'd snuck into their restricted area to see the red-spot alert on my leg. I had gone through this ordeal of being stripped, scanned and questioned four times before, but never did they ask me about any medical device in my leg. If they were so concerned about it, why not ask me?

Of course, I wasn't aware I had a medical device in my leg. Nor did my parents know of any implant.

You might assume that since then I would have gone to see a doctor to get it checked out, but I haven't. Why not? First of all, I am not bothered by it. Second, I already know by *intuition* that doctors won't find anything and won't waste my time in pursuits that will not yield results. Why won't they find anything? Because the Israeli scanners are of an entirely different caliber than those of other airports, surpassing the instruments of doctors. If anyone is going to find that piece, then it's the most suspicious security team on the planet: the Tel Aviv airport. The country of Israel itself, is a high-security facility. Every inch of the country is wired, bugged, tapered with electric fences and monitored by more cameras than all the Hollywood studios combined.

Remembering those incidents now, they always followed the same pattern. My presence caused consternation with the security officers there. There would be a lot of telephoning, a lot of walking back and forth. More superior border agents would then come and question me. And then what appeared to be even more superior agents, dressed in civilian clothing, would come and take a look at me. Each of the five times I went through this ordeal, I'd be taken to a cabin and asked to undress. My clothing would be scanned. Every single item in my luggage would be scrutinized. Several officers would interview me, sometimes at the same time. They seemed uneasy with whatever they thought I was doing, being or carrying with me. Then senior staff would appear, scan my legs with devices of their own. Then they would close the curtain, leaving me standing there half nude. The senior officers would reassure the security staff that all is somehow well and the regular staff would come back, tell me to get dressed and, satisfied that I had no clue what they were after, let me go.

Once, the whole procedure took so long that I missed a flight. Perhaps it also had something to do with the fact that on three of my five visits to Israel, I traversed the border to Palestine, having seminar business to conduct there. Some of their questions seemed to imply that I liked Palestinians and disliked Jews. But the truth is, if I have the opportunity to teach my seminars, I don't care whether someone is a Jew, a Palestinian or anything else for that matter. And I have in fact conducted one seminar for Israelis before, in the city of Tel Aviv. That was during my first visit to Israel, but it resulted in the very same scrutiny of my leg, stripping, full body search and interview with multiple worried officers. In retrospect, it seemed they knew something about me that I didn't know about myself.

A Strange Sexual Encounter

My newfound curiosity revealed several other episodes from my life that appeared to have a deeper meaning than I thought at the time, especially the strange manner of the very first time I had sex. Back then, I thought nothing of it other than that I'd been lucky. But in retrospect I see there was nothing *normal* about any of it. I was fifteen years old and the girl was also fifteen. She appeared out of nowhere as a new classmate who had "just moved to town". After she had made love to me, she just so happened to "move out of town" again.

Through fields of wheat I rode home from school on my bike every day. It just so happened that she took the same way home on her bike, as I discovered when I caught up to her slow pace. For a few weeks, it was only me and her out in those fields after school. I had been alone out there for months, and now I had a companion.

At that time, my book shelves were full of books about aliens, UFOs, ancient aliens, etc. At age fifteen, that was my biggest fascination, not women. But she hadn't seen my library, nor had I dared bring those topics up while with her. My teenage mind thought that attractive girls and UFO books didn't mix. The guys that were liked by girls then were not into books, they were into sports. Of course, later in life, the bookish guys, not the muscle guys get the best women, but I didn't understand that at the time.

She was the most dazzling girl I had ever met. With soft facial features, long blonde curly hair, a small nose and light blue eyes, she looked out of place compared to the other kids. She was also dressed in a peculiar manner. I remember feeling poorly dressed beside her. While I wore random sneakers, shorts and a t-shirt, she looked as if were dressed by some kind of aristocratic mother.

She brought up the subject of aliens, ancient aliens and UFOs on her own, without having seen my bookshelf.

"Wow, you're into that too?" I asked, feeling both surprised and impressed.

Looking back, I realize it was all a little too convenient, like some kind of staged fairy tale. The best-looking girl I had ever seen, just so happened to move to my town, have the same way home as me, "coincidentally" also liked alien-topics and just so happened to move away after we have sex. My teenage-self was easily fooled.

One day I invited her to my place knowing my parents were not home. I had rarely ever had a female visitor at my place, was shy to let anyone know and also worried they might not approve. Even though we had talked about aliens incessantly on our way home, once we arrived in my room, she wasn't at all interested in the books I was trying to show her. She had come with the singular agenda and purpose: to have sex with me. And she told me so, as she dragged me into bed.

She said something strange. Looking back on it now, it almost sounded like out of some cheesy romantic sci-fi: "We will have sex now. After that, you will not see me again. I want you to know, that it's not because of you. I like you."

I asked, "Why won't we see each other again? I don't mind if we do." That was an understatement.

She responded something like, "I can't explain right now. You'll understand one day." Since I didn't want to ruin the moment, I didn't dwell on it.

I then made love for the first time. It was not her first time though. I guess it's typical that the first time, the experience was not entirely relaxed, but because I was enamored by her, it was not unpleasant either. Strangely enough she had tears in her eyes while we made love. I didn't question her on that either.

In fact, today I realize there is *a whole lot that I didn't question.* I've always been the naively optimistic guy who didn't overanalyze. That's what has kept me happy.

Then, as if her entire mission were accomplished and her charade over, she got dressed and left. She in fact left so quickly, I was taken aback. I wished to discuss some books with her, but she had no interest. I asked to accompany her home, but she wouldn't let me. I had never seen her home and didn't even know where she lived. In fact, I never saw her again!

She disappeared entirely. She did not show up at school. When I asked around, nobody seemed to know where she lived. Wanting to see her again, I even asked the school teacher about her. She told me that she had "moved". Normally, I wouldn't press other people's private issues at that young age, but I insisted to know more.

"But didn't she just move here a few weeks ago?"

"Yes. It's strange, isn't it? Now she has moved again." The teacher didn't seem to understand either.

I thought that she might still be packing up or something and rode my bike around town to see if I might see her. It was a small town, adjacent to a city. The field we rode on every day separated the city from the village. Where riding on those fields used to feel beautiful and free, now the trip felt lonely — because I had known it riding with her.

The first time our class teacher called out her name, I had actually memorized it. Why? Because I had liked her from the first moment. So, I looked up her name in the phonebook (there was no internet in those days). I didn't find it. It occurred to me that a fifteen-year-old would probably not be listed. So, I looked up her last name and found about ten entries, but none of them lived anywhere near my city or even region, much less the small suburb we rode to.

A few years ago, still curious, I typed her name into Google, Facebook and a few other places. I found nothing. Not a single person in the world with that name. That was really odd because the name didn't sound that rare. I found plenty of people with her first name or her last name, but none with both. So I looked people up with that last name in that area. I found nobody even remotely resembling her. *Under that name, no person existed.* The name that was given to the school, did not exist.

A beautiful girl comes out of nowhere, gives a false name, instantly targets Fred, lures him by talking about aliens, sleeps with him, then disappears never to be seen or heard of again. Not only that, but she announces — before sex — that "I cannot see you again, but some day you will understand why". Upon writing this story down for this book, it is now obvious that there is more going on. When she said "someday I will understand why", she was practically announcing that something was going on in secret. And then there were her tears. So, was this encounter merely to collect my seed, similar to the blood sample event?

It feels odd to me that various people would just come to collect my sperm and blood without telling me anything about it. It feels odd that there are people who appear to know more about me than myself. To this day, I do not understand what happened there, but if her promise comes true, one day I will.

The Serpent

Even though the ostensible Pleiadeans did not tell me who they were paying to get my DNA, I intuitively sensed it. It was a race of interdimensional beings I call "The Serpent" in this book. It is they who temporarily and illegally rule this planet.

It seemed they didn't want to tell me, and by suppressing those thoughts, I picked up on them (trying to hide thoughts by resisting them, actually amplifies them. If one really wanted to hide thoughts, they shouldn't even start thinking them). Humans are not inherently inferior to many of these extraterrestrials. Being able to pick up thoughts they were trying to mask, reminded me of that fact. One of the greatest impediments to human potential is our own inferiority complex. Abilities such as telepathy, Intuition, remote perception, healing, remote healing and many others are native to you, but this you were not taught in "school".

Apart from the Pleiadeans, the Serpent are the other class of beings I encountered in early childhood. I have written about these extraterrestrial or extradimensional beings in my books on ancient Atlantis. We have a long history with them. I wrote about my childhood encounters with them in my book, *Journeys in Spectral Consciousness*. But when I wrote that book, it was not entirely clear to me who they were or that they might be the mortal enemy of another people from the Pleiades. Nor did I know that they owned the Earth (if the information I picked up telepathically, is correct).

But perhaps it was already clear to me at a subconscious level. At the early age of thirteen, I had been drawn to all sorts of conspiracy literature, including the books of David Icke, who famously (or infamously) wrote that the Earth is secretly governed by the "Illuminati" who are, in reality, extraterrestrial Reptilians. I now see that I had been drawn to that literature at such an early age in order to make sense of what was already stored in my subconscious.

Between the ages of thirteen and twenty-two, I read just about every book on "conspiracies" available. But that didn't satisfy me. The literature induced a sense of darkness and despair. It always referred to "everything being under control", every supposed positive being a deception of the negative, so that in the end you even had to suspect the local baker, postal office worker or plumber of being "in on it". I mocked this type of thinking as "low consciousness" and "fear-based".

I was always an upbeat person and couldn't identify with the idea of doom and gloom. Through my own efforts, I have created a very positive life for myself, so how could it be true that we live in a mass delusion? At around the age of twenty-two, I renounced conspiracy theories and embraced the Law of Attraction, which essentially states just the opposite: Rather than being victims of overwhelming evil, we are each solely responsible for the reality we create.

It doesn't pay off to feel like a victim. In fact, much of that kind of information just isn't healthy. However, that doesn't mean deception, cover-up and evil intent don't exist. It just means that I don't feel victimized by it. I feel great joy and exhilaration for the future of humankind.

Evil does exist, but we do not have to vibrate on its frequency. And in this way, we can sidestep its influence. Nonetheless, there is something to this whole "Reptilian" thing as espoused by David Icke and many other conspiracy researchers. *Every single* religion and mythological account tells of the wars between the Serpent and their foes in some form or another. So, while I tell you about it, please keep in mind that, while it's true, you needn't ever have anything to do with it. If you know that love neutralizes fear, nothing negative will ever have power over you.

At the age of approximately four, I would scream in utter horror at their visitations. I would wake up with actual physical bite marks on my body. It was at that point that my mother was convinced I wasn't merely having nightmares but actual visitations or what she called "demonic attacks". Night by night I would complain that "monsters" were coming and taking me away. For some reason, my parents would not let me sleep in their bedroom, so I felt vulnerable and exposed to these intensely hateful creatures. That's how they appeared to me as a child: a pure manifestation of hate.

Now, at a more mature age, I do not fear them, I have compassion for them because I now see that they try to scare children, because they themselves are afraid. Rather than being all-powerful evil, as conspiracy theorists and religious preachers say, they are *weak* when it comes to higher realms. The only humans they have power over are humans that are terrified.

They took me on journeys to their world, which appeared to be inside of our Earth and also within the interior of other planets, including a red desert planet that was probably Mars. They showed me their worlds. I remember not liking the trips. Protesting them. Throwing a fit. And being *forced* by them. They love forcing defenseless people. Why they singled me out for visitation and attack, I don't know. But in retrospect, I'd say that it matured me rather rapidly. I'd already started questioning life as a toddler. If you're repeatedly thrown into rotten and nauseating scenarios against your will, you'll start questioning things too. The places they took me to looked grim, muddy, deserted, burning, rugged or rough, as if the landscapes of the planets reflect the mentality of their inhabitants.

At the early age of four, to ward off these creatures, my mother taught me to pray. And pray I did. The attacks subsided. Realizing that prayer worked gave me tremendous confidence as a child. I felt like all I had to do was intend for something deeply and it came true. Having been formed at the age of four, I still use this today, and it always works like magic. Just to be clear: I haven't set foot into a church in decades and do not belong to any particular religion. The power behind prayer does not derive from a particular religion or denomination or belief-system, it comes from one's own trust and faith in a Higher Power.

My father told me the following story: One night he woke up to go to the bathroom. As he entered the hallway, he saw a bright light emanating from my bedroom. At first, he stood frozen in shock, knowing that no lamp or lightbulb could produce rays of that intensity. But looking at them for a while had a calming effect on him, so he quietly approached my room. He said he saw four very tall "angels" standing around my bed. Not wanting to disturb them, he snuck back to bed and went to sleep in peace. I believe those angel visitations made the attacks stop.

I don't know why I was attacked in the first place. One of the strange quirks of life on Earth is that we experience all kinds of hardship that only stop when we demand or call for it to stop. If we fail to specifically request it, it often just keeps playing out. What this means is that we have the power to start and stop certain realities and that perhaps we had a role in their starting. Maybe I had some unresolved karma with them from another life, place or time. Or maybe they just like harassing the defenseless.

Years later, at around the age of twelve, I had recurring vivid dreams of reptilian creatures. Those dreams inspired me to take notes. I never thought these notes would one day make their way into a book. I wrote the notes and hid them in between my books because I didn't want my parents or friends to think there was something wrong with me. I recovered these notes when I was nineteen years old. Since I was planning to sell all of my books at a garage sale, I paged through them and found the notes. I re-read them and then threw them away. But I remember the dreams and the descriptions of them clearly to this day.

I saw their life in caverns beneath the Earth's crust. I saw their spaceships coming and going from below the Earth, through holes in the Antarctic and various deserts in Australia, Arabia, the Caucasus Region and places I couldn't identify. Based on these vision-like dreams, I'd look at maps of the Australian desert with spellbound fascination. If there was a documentary of, say, Kazakhstan, I'd watch with eyes wide open. Those dreams were stored in my subconscious my entire life.

I saw elevators in big cities leading to their world underground. I saw massive subterranean subway systems nobody knows about. I saw them taking on their more common astral-energy bodies and hovering above and behind people's shoulders, manipulating their actions. I saw all this and much more, wrote it down, but chose to ignore it until recently. Ignoring it was good, because I have led a happy life and have not been bothered by them throughout adulthood.

Conspiracy writers claim that these Reptilians shapeshift to take on the form of humans and politicians. I didn't see that and I can't confirm it. There are countless YouTube videos and books talking about shapeshifting Reptilians, but that's not the way I perceive them. To me, their influence is subtle, psychic, astral.

When you travel throughout Asia, you see their statues everywhere. Even when you travel in Europe, you see their dragon statues guarding towns. In fact, there is no place in the world where you won't see some of their symbolism. So, if they are not real on some level, then why are they firmly ingrained in our collective consciousness? They are real. But from my vantage point they are no more dangerous than insects. Why is that? Because a level of consciousness at "level 5" (on a scale from 1 to 10) is so vastly different from a "level 2" that the two realities never intersect, just like a fish will never intersect with a mountain goat. The fish lives in the water; the goat lives on a mountain. The fish need not be afraid of the goat because the goat, by nature, does not venture into water. So, the only real influence the reptilian species has on humans is through the non-physical. Can they take possession of a physical body? Yes, I believe so. But even this could only be done with the consent of the human, never against their will.

Bloodlines

Remembering events around my DNA, taking blood samples and sperm got me thinking about another event from my life that I was able to reframe for this book. Of course, at the time I again "thought nothing of it" and just went about my life as if everything were normal. It's funny how oblivious I have been to things going on around me. I've been conducting "Awareness Training" to individuals and companies my entire life, all the while being blissfully unaware of events in my own life. The beauty of it all is that there seems to be no limit to things one could become aware of. I believe that I were to focus on the stories told in this book even more deeply, even more layers would reveal themselves.

I was around twenty-six when I was sent to the island of Malta to do a seminar on behalf of a training company. I was to teach these people NLP or something of that sort (back then this training company sent me to do seminars on all sorts of topics, regardless of whether I knew them or not, simply because I was an entertaining speaker). I was told that I'd be working with "billionaires" and "very influential people" and to show proper respect and decorum. For instance, I wasn't to conduct my training in sneakers and I was told not to ask about their private affairs or even ask their names. I was told that I shouldn't even learn their real names. Instead, everyone should make up new names and that this would be a "playful NLP exercise". It was not the first time they had sent me to work with extremely wealthy people and I was used to it by then. Wealth didn't mean anything to me and I never treated the wealthy any different than I treated regular folk, hence it didn't make me apprehensive or nervous.

Some of the wealthy I worked with were very kind and warm-hearted people, some were assholes. In fact, I've noticed that good and bad are more extreme among the wealthy. That's because money does not change people, it shows who they are. Those with money tend to express themselves more brazenly because they needn't fear repercussions or financial survival. So, among the rich you have more very good and very bad, whereas among "normal folk" people are normally a mix of the two.

In this instance, I found it difficult to respect the people I was working with. The moment they entered the training room, I *instantly* realized that they were all involved in *extreme crime*. Call it psychic intuition or just experience, I could feel it at once. These were not the "wealthy people" I had been expecting.

Standing in front of a group of eight people, I could sense violence, prostitution, arms dealing, drug running, human trafficking and even murder. All of them were covered in tattoos showing allegiance to skulls, snakes, crosses, numbers and other symbols. The seminar was to go four days, but I could hardly handle spending just a few minutes with these people. It's weird how crime leaves a spiritual *stench* that can easily be sensed. I didn't know anything about them, but felt their entire history. They were sitting there acting as if they were regular people like anyone else, but their charade was ridiculous. There is something strangely moronic about violent criminals, as if half of their brain capacity is out of order and they have a hard time learning new things. I certainly didn't want to spend time with them. And they were visibly uneasy with me as well.

I thank Hollywood movies for teaching me how to deal with people like this. I showed no hint of fear. As you know from the movies, the moment you show fear, they want to hurt you. As explained earlier (and as I will repeat again later because it's an important survival technique), evil people have so much suppressed fear that they only dare attack people who are themselves afraid. A fearless person impresses them at a spiritual level.

I went about the business of doing a seminar I had done a few times before. I'm usually able to break the ice and elicit a few chuckles from students within the first fifteen minutes, but these folks just had a paranoid glare, as if they were waiting and ready to be assaulted at any minute. So I had to change my approach and started talking about how NLP can be used for manipulation and how teaching them about that will prevent them from being manipulated. Predictably, they lit up on this topic, but only a little. We spent the whole day doing exercises on manipulation, under the guise of preventing it.

By the end of the first day, I was able to turn the atmosphere from tense to a bit of a vacation feeling. I realized that none of these people had a regular life and didn't even know how to behave in a civilized manner. I saw them more as victims than criminals. In fact, I learned that most perpetrators were, at one point in their lives, also victims. Sitting around or being quiet for too long, they would fidget and their eyes would start nervously jumping amongst each other. There shouldn't be any relaxation because that means they would have to face the utter mess that their existence had become. I frantically had to move from one activity to the next to keep them busy.

On the second day, we did a few communication techniques and some belief work. That is extremely difficult, if not impossible, with people who are bottling up endless traumatic emotions and vile transgressions against others. It meant that the belief-changing work could only take place within a very limited compartment of their overall persona and no doors to the subconscious could be opened. Their level of cognition was almost moronic. How could these people possibly be "billionaires" unless through fraud and theft? For example, I was explaining to them how they could find out whether a woman's attention was on them or not.

"Check if the front of her shoe soles are pointed at you," I told them, which was one of ten subconscious cues.

Then one of them said, "But if she's not looking at me, how should I know whether the shoe pointing at me, means her attention is on me?"

I said, "Its subconscious. The feet generally point to the person we are thinking of, like some kind of antenna."

He said, "But if she is not looking at me, I wouldn't know."

I responded, "Well, check in different situations. Maybe you're standing in a circle of people and notice her feet pointing at you. Then later, you're sitting in the living room and her feet again happen to be pointing at you. Then, a week later, the same thing. Regardless of whether she is looking at you are not, chances are high you are on her mind."

Then he said, "But how can I be on her mind if she's not looking at me?"

At this point his colleagues mocked him for not getting it. That's the level of intelligence I was dealing with. I was frustrated and really just wanted to finish the seminar as quickly as possible. The company required me to work with these idiots.

At the end of the second day, their boss — a blonde haired muscle-guy with sailor tattoos all over his arms, piercing blue eyes — insisted that I go "have a beer" with him. I declined, but he wouldn't let me go. "Just one beer. Come on." It seemed urgent to him. In fact, it's difficult to say "No" to a person you feel is about to beat the living daylights out of you deny their request.

The minute we sat down, he started, "I'm not going to beat around the bush. Have you heard of the Teutonic Knights?" He had expectant eyes, as if I knew exactly what he was talking about, but I actually had no idea. Nor did I care. I just wanted to get away. His vibe was aggressive, as if there were an underlying rage that could instantly turn into cold blooded murder at any hint of disapproval from my side. He then explained that the "Teutonic Knights" were a "secret society" and that they were protecting the world from evil. He said they'd existed for thousands of years. "I'm telling you this because I was wondering if you are interested in joining."

As a teenager I had read just about every book on secret societies I could get my hands on, but I had never heard of "Teutonic Knights". A decade later, looking it up on the internet, I found nothing on them in relation to modern crime on the island of Malta. The revelation was surprising as it was unappealing. Not only did I not believe that these were "the good guys fighting evil", but I didn't want to be put in a situation where I had to reject a potential psychopath that might not take my rejection lightly. He claimed that their "honorable organization" was founded in Malta thousands of years ago, operated from Malta, controlled Malta and many other "regions" in the world. I didn't respond to his question about joining. Instead, I asked questions, just to postpone the inevitable. I asked about other secret societies. He said,

"No, we're much bigger than that." Yet it was clear to me that someone who had to *boast* about his secret club, didn't have much of a club. I got the distinct vibe that he actually felt insecure in my presence and was trying to cover up his shortcomings by posing as someone who had something to offer. If he indeed was a member of this powerful organization, I didn't for a second believe that he had any position of significance or high standing in it.

Then I had an idea about how to get out of this: I could tell him I'm interested and go to bed, finish the seminar in two days, fly home and just never call back. So, I feigned interest. "Wow, that's interesting."

He showed me one of his tattoos, supposedly part of his initiation. The tattoos broadcast more of a mafia-like organization than a traditional esoteric society.

The reason I remember the story in this context is because he said something surprising to me that I didn't understand: "I know it's for you Fred. You're from the X family, man (family name removed and replaced by" X" for privacy purposes)."

Again, there was the appearance of someone knowing something about me that I didn't know. This seemed to be one of the patterns of my life. At first, I thought that "You're from the X family" referred to some slang or saying by him that I was not privy too. I pondered over it for a while after going back to my hotel room. What does it mean to be "from the X family"? At the time I did not relate it to me at all because *I didn't know my ancestors had that name.* I could tell he could see that I didn't understand, so he didn't tell me more about it either. After about an hour of this bizarreness, I said I wanted to go prepare the next seminar day then go to sleep.

The hotel was at the ocean, so I went outside to stare out into it and ponder upon the meeting. Having a sickish feeling in my stomach, I wanted nothing to do with these people and at that point I decided that I would *abandon* the seminar and fly home.

Was I being too hard and judgmental with them? No. It's hard to describe non-physical vibes in words. There was no compatibility between me and them, and I didn't belong there.

I didn't want to explain myself, didn't want to let them know, didn't want to apologize. I just wanted to get as far away from them as I could. Never in my life had I come that close to palpable evil. Looking into the guy's eyes and listening to his words, I detected not the slightest trace of humor, compassion, patience or tolerance. It was truly nerve-racking to just be *near* people like this, not to mention having them in a seminar.

There was a worry that the training company would not re-book me if I abandoned their event, but I cared more for my well-being than for the money. I also began questioning the training company itself. My boss not only did business with these crooks but asked me not to mention their names. This indicated to me, that he deliberately did business with them even though he knew about their background. I made a few intention affirmations out into the ocean that all would be well and went back to my room to sleep.

The next day, what happened was even more amazing than what had already happened. I didn't have to abandon the seminar. The boss of the training company was in the lobby. Police officers were there. The blonde "Teutonic Knights" guy I had had a beer with the night earlier was in front of the hotel in handcuffs! And what was my boss doing there? Had he flown in? I hadn't seen him in a while and suddenly he appeared out of nowhere. He asked me to sit down. He told me the seminar had been cancelled but that I'd get paid the full amount anyway. He told me that three of my students had been arrested in relation to organized crime!

As shaken as I was, I also felt triumphant over the fact that I had known it all along. I told my boss that I knew something wasn't right about them. What I didn't mention was that I also knew there was something very strange about my boss, but that's another story for another time. I was shaken because I had been among high-level criminals, my life perhaps in danger.

"You have nothing to worry about. They didn't take your name," my boss said, referring to the police. They had been strangely tense and aggressive during our two days of training. Maybe they sensed their time was up.

The *most* amazing part of the story happened months later, when my mother told me that her father, whom I had never known because he died young, was a Greek man by the name of X and that they were apparently a "very wealthy and famous family". I immediately remembered what the handcuffed "Teutonic Knight" had said to me on that peculiar evening: "You are from the X family!"

I did not tell my mother the story. I kept it to myself because — how are you going to explain that to anyone? I didn't want to unnecessarily worry her with mafia stories. So how could this guy possibly know that I am descendant from that family — even I didn't know it. The training company I worked for didn't know it. But some criminal on the island of Malta knew it and, on that basis, wanted me in his secret society?

Just what was going on here? I spent a few days speculating. Do these people have a database of bloodlines by which they choose their members? Do they evaluate people based on their bloodline? Had someone — again — taken my blood sample and evaluated it? Or did he have psychic-astral means to get information out of me? Or did his crime network do a background check on me before I arrived?

At first, I found the third explanation the most probable. They have to be careful who they hang out with. Police are looking for them, so they have secret databases on which they run background checks on everyone. That may or may not be true, but upon further deliberation, I realized that the family name seemed really important to him, and the basis of inviting me into his organization. So apparently, membership is related to bloodline. That is why, while editing this book, I removed that family name and replaced it with "X". I wouldn't want other weirdos showing up in my life on that basis.

Did I go research this "X" family? I didn't, actually. It doesn't interest me. I do not define myself physically but spiritually. I do not personally know a single member of this family, am not interested in knowing them and do not believe I can "find something out about myself" through genealogy. I understand that bloodlines and family name are very important for many people out there, but they aren't for me. I have met quite a few people with a "good family name" who are not good people but believe they are good because of their "name".

A family name or bloodline is meaningless. Biological heritage is only important to those who have forgotten their unique souls and that they can *create* who they would like to be in life. So, no, I did not "look up" "who I am" because that is not who I am. In fact, I recall my mother obsessing for years over her own "racial heritage" and her "ancestors", but I do not recall it having gotten her anywhere in life. Of what use is having a "good name" if you don't have a good game?

Secret Libraries

There are secret libraries that are neither open nor even known to the public. The set of knowledge for the general public, is not the same set of knowledge certain elect circles are privileged with. At some intuitive level I have always known this (hence my lifelong search for better knowledge), but about ten years ago, I was actually fortunate enough to see for myself. Sharing all the knowledge I do, it is no coincidence that I attract people who share knowledge with me. We get back what we put out into the world.

This particular experience was not ambivalent or doubtful. I was wide awake and aware of it being an extraordinary event while it was happening.

I was conducting a coaching session in the mansion of another very rich person. Strictly speaking, it wasn't "coaching". The man merely wanted to sit with me and discuss metaphysics and philosophy, but it was booked as coaching. This man only booked me once, and I did not see him again after. Rather than having an assistant book me, as was often the case among the busy, he wrote to me directly and offered to have me flown to his country. I ran his name through an internet search, but there was nothing on him. So, he either provided a false name or he just wasn't publicly known.

We sat for three hours drinking coffee and talking. I enjoyed the conversation because he knew exactly what he wanted to talk about. Asking me these questions had been worth thousands of dollars to him. He seemed overjoyed at discussing sophisticated topics, as if those around him did not share his enthusiasm for the esoteric.

The impression he made on me was as though he was from another century. Although English was not his native language, he used vocabulary much more refined and specific than in common usage. He had written down certain quotes from my books and was especially interested in *where* I got specific information. So, I explained to him my process of intuition, experience and research I used to put together a book. But he kept digging in a curious way for very specific points of information, some of which I didn't even remember. In cases I did remember, he scribbled notes on his sheet of paper.

For example, he'd point at a certain paragraph from one of my books (which were strangely worn, as if they had been read by many) and said, "Did you get this from Meister Eckart?" At the time I had never heard of anyone called Meister Eckhart.

I replied, "No. It just occurred to me, based on what I was writing about."

He then asked, "Have you ever read Meister Eckhart? Because Eckhart said the exactly same thing."

I assured him I had never heard the name before. Later, looking it up on Wikipedia, I learned that Meister Eckhart was a "German theologian, philosopher and mystic" who was born in 1260 and tried has a heretic by the Pope.

That's how the entire three hours went. He'd look at his sheet, ask a question or make a comment and drop all kinds of names I had never heard of and inquire of things I myself did not fully understand. Most people underestimate the scope of my knowledge, but this guy clearly overestimated it. On several occasions he made references to things I did not understand.

The house was big, but when he gave me a tour, I noticed that I hadn't seen half of the place. I soon found out that the other half contained a secret library. My host introduced it with, "I'll show you something that will interest you very much."

What looked like a high wall with intricate etching and woodcuts, opened at the push of a button, activated from another room. My only reference for such a thing was Hollywood movies. As the wall opened, it revealed a vaulted door, similar to that of a high-security bank! Just seeing that, I knew that what he was going to show me was apparently very important. He opened the vault himself and motioned me to step through it. When I realized what I was seeing, I felt humbled. The library was bigger than most public libraries I had seen. It was vast and must have had at least thirty rows of book and manuscript shelving reaching to a very high ceiling. At first that didn't make sense to me, because the house didn't seem that high from the outside. Then I realized we had gone down stairs two floors to reach it. There were high ladders and the lights were dimmed. I knew then and there, before even seeing a single book, that something profound, rare, outside of everyday-life reality was happening.

As we walked the library, he explained to me that this book collection could be worth billions. He asked me not to touch any of the books because it would sound off an alarm that he hadn't deactivated. He also claimed that none of the books were public and many of them weren't even known to exist. They had no "International Standard Book Number", often no recognizable publisher and many of the authors were anonymous or used pen names. A few of them looked new, but most of them were well worn and even antique. I was allowed to walk around and read some of the book titles. Truly, I did not find a *single title* I recognized. Some of the books were bound, some existed as paper bindings or manuscripts. Those bound sometimes had strange symbols on them. The place felt alien and fascinating, as if it were an example of a parallel reality existing alongside the everyday reality of the average Joe.

I memorized some of the book titles in my mind, so that I could internet search them later when I got home. I couldn't find a single trace of any of them on the internet. Imagine that! I had memorized four book titles, but as far as the "all knowing" internet was concerned, they didn't exist! I won't share them here because I got the urgent impression that my host takes the secrecy of his library and books quite seriously.

But here is the strangest thing about the book titles: The topics were so foreign that it looked and felt as if they were written based on an entirely different paradigm than ours. It was like strolling through a library on another planet that doesn't share the same understanding of reality. Before reading any of those books, I'd need re-education on what life is. If you walk through a normal public library, you have different sections: Sports, Romance, Sci-Fi, Self-Help, Crafts, History, War, Travel, Religion, New Age, Entertainment, etc. The books I saw in this library didn't fit any category I knew. Some of were vaguely recognizable as esoteric metaphysical books, but most of them defied labeling.

"WTF IS THIS!" was my predominant thought. It reminded me of the infamous Voynich Manuscript, a mysterious booklet full of illustrations and language nobody understood, except, the entire library was full of books like this. I did recognize some English language titles as well as other known languages, but there were also book cover writings containing symbols that didn't look like any known language. Most of the English language titles I did understand, looked bizarre. Some of them didn't make sense to me. If I asked you to separate chalkboard carriages further up the monkey hill, before the final moon-gown laughs its trebled ricochet haven for the elderly radio set, would you understand what I'm talking about? I didn't think so. And that's how I felt in that library. I liked it a lot because not understanding anything means there is a lot to learn. That puts us back into a child-like state in which the whole world is mysterious and we will one day understand and, as a result, be able to experience a whole lot more.

The tour was over too soon. I'd have gladly spent several weeks only in that hall, educating myself on this other reality.

I told my host that I had never seen anything like it and thanked him for showing me. He didn't ask me to keep it secret, but it was implied in the context. I didn't ask him why he kept this hidden because the answer was intuitively obvious. It would have been like asking why I don't make an iPhone available to a group of cats. Some things are just not compatible.

I think he may have shown me the library out of curiosity. To see whether I would write about it, what I would say about it if I do or whether I would keep it to myself. Well, I have kept it to myself for over a decade now. But now I wrote about it. So there you go.

That day was the first and last time I visited that particular house and the only time I saw a secret library. I never talked about it because I didn't know what to make of it or how to describe it. From a reductionist viewpoint, one could simply say that I visited the private library of an eccentric man who liked to collect obscure writings. But it was more than that. It was a high-security, alarm-protected library full of unknown books that were written for an entirely different set of society. It amazes me that there are groups of people out there who occupy an entirely different world and yet share the same planet with us.

I also hesitated talking or writing about this because people might insist to see it, know where it is, or ask more about it. But rest assured, I have nothing more than this to share about it. It's some rich guy's private collection of obscure books. Such libraries exist. That's all I know. If you wish to see for yourself, then attract it into your life.

Throughout the years, I have often done internet searches for "secret library" and similar terms, but found nothing even remotely close to what I saw. I've always thought search engines contained all information I'd ever need. But it would appear that the amount of knowledge we have yet to acquire, is unlimited.

There are many more tales from my life that I will tell over time, once they become clearer to me. What I know while writing this is that there is so much I do not know. Some of it I don't really want to know, for the sake of my own peace. And much of it I am learning to my great delight. Life is so much more amazing than many of us assume.

CHAPTER FOUR

TYPES OF ANGELS, ENTITIES AND EXTRATERRESTRIALS

The multiverse is populated by so many different physical and non-physical beings that one person could never know them all. Rather than classifying them by race, one could classify them by whether they are friendly or not from a human perspective. There are those at a lower consciousness that we would consider malevolent. Of the malevolent forces that are of peripheral interest to us are those *living inside the Earth,* below the ground you walk on. I realize it sounds like science-fiction, even pulp sci-fi that an ancient space-faring race of interdimensional and extraterrestrial beings live in the interior of the planet and that spaceships come and go from the inner Earth into deep space on a daily basis. As crazy as this may sound, every ancient mythology and religion from around the globe and almost every single culture points to this very thing. As I mentioned previously, this race of beings are historically known as "The Serpent" in Abrahamic religions, the Nagas (aquatic reptiles) in Buddhism, or the dragon in Native American and Asian tales.

You might be surprised to learn that the Serpent is not the only race of beings living inside Earth. Once your awareness expands, you will learn that throughout the Universe, it is not uncommon to live inside planets rather than on their surface. Does that sound strange to you? If so, consider that you yourself prefer living sheltered in a house rather than outdoors. The interior of Earth also houses a race of dwarves, that I have described in previous books and a sprinkling of other civilizations.

Some extraterrestrial races that come to Earth to visit, ignore surface-dwellers, assuming that "Planet Earth" mostly takes place in its interior — while you probably think that the surface of the Earth features the pinnacle of civilized life in the Universe. Maybe this seems unbelievable to you and you don't want to take my word for it. If so, you might want to start looking into this at a more scientific and grounded level. I recommend books by Richard Sauder Ph.D. That author has written several books, meticulously documenting and proving the U.S. Government construction of subterranean and underwater cities, facilities, military bases housing millions of personnel and people. Believe it or not, 99% of humanity is unaware of that fact. Now if we are not even aware of that provable fact, how much more are we unaware of? Once you have looked into that, research mythological accounts of trips into the "Underworld". The ancients called the inner Earth "Underworld", an endless system of tunnels, caverns and habitations below Earth. It is only in modern times that the cult of Scientism has redefined the meaning of the Underworld to mean "a place in the afterlife". The problem with this manipulative reframing is that the ancients had separate words for afterlife and underworld wasn't one of them.

Yes, one can travel to the underworld in the afterlife, in one's spiritual or astral body, but the place referenced in ancient religions and cultural legends is clearly the interior of Earth. Just like there has been an effort to mask the nature of reality and the existence of extraterrestrials, there has also been great effort to mask the existence of subterranean civilizations.

Once you become aware of the U.S. military efforts to inhabit the inner Earth and are aware of what the ancients have to say about it, you can expand your studies to include the Nazis attempted penetration of subterranean lands, the existence of Buddhist scriptures on underground cities as well as the tales of thousands of people who accidentally stumbled upon them during their hikes, cave explorations and their geological scanning.

Just because people are too lazy to research something, doesn't mean it doesn't exist. Those who cover these things up don't put that much effort into their cover up because they know most humans don't really bother using their innate powers of attention to investigate. Hence, you only know the truths you deserve to know.

Then there are those aliens at high consciousness, which we would experience as benevolent. The reason I say that "we would experience" various beings as good and evil, is because our own level of consciousness is not all that high. From the highest vantage point, the "villains" are not solely "evil" for the sake of evil, but follow a particular cosmic plan. Or put it differently: When you walk on a footpath and crush a group of ants, destroying a village of anthills with your boots, *to these ants* you are malevolent or evil, but that's not your view of the situation. The construction worker using a dredge to remove soil probably does not consider himself malevolent, but all the creatures that lived there probably would (if they had awareness of good vs. evil). Likewise, the beings that are evil or dangerous to us, simply don't care one bit about our well-being, consider us nothing more than pesky bugs. They do not consider themselves evil.

Many of these "benevolent" beings are also neutral toward us or, frankly, disinterested. Some have a benevolent attitude toward us in specific, but wouldn't necessarily rush to our assistance. This is not much different from Earth, where you might have a benevolent attitude toward some distant tribe living in the Amazonian rainforest. But just because you feel good about them wouldn't mean you'd actually travel there, interact with them or even assist them when they are facing a crisis. You'd expect them to help themselves. There might be the odd anthropologist, social worker, wisdom-seeker or adventurer who shows up in their village, but most of us have our own stuff to attend to. Aliens feel similar.

That's not to say we are on entirely on our own. There are a select few that have overwhelming love and protectiveness toward humanity. Who are they? They are those who have ancestry on Earth and those who were involved in the creation of this planet and our bodies, as well as non-physical beings who understand our long-term role in the grand scheme of things. Just like on Earth, we have greater love and protective instincts toward our own children. Just like we would never allow anyone to harm our children, they would never allow anyone to harm us if they can avoid it.

If you came to understand that this Amazonian tribe is not just some primitive culture with nothing to offer, but rather holders of an ancient secret who have a positive spiritual influence on the planet, you might gain a different appreciation of them than the thrill-seeking tourist would. The telltale sign of higher consciousness then is simply *care*. The sign of lower consciousness is lack of *care*.

I dedicated an entire book — *Lives of the Soul* — to the positive beings up there. Just one of these beings could easily fix all of humanity's problems in just a single day. It would be a snap. Such a higher consciousness being could voice a single intention, and *all would be healed at once*. I have experienced and witnessed these powers. But the fact that they don't use these powers, should tell us something about the deeper purpose of Earth and our life on it. If Earth were, at this time, meant to be saved, it would be. It isn't, because it's our job to do that, not theirs. How? Through increased energy, care and creativity. Our problems are not that big that we are unable to solve them ourselves. Relying on others to fix them, only delays them. Imagine seeing an eight-year-old child that fell off a bike. The child, uninjured, would be easily able to brush off his pants, adjust the bike handle and continue riding it. But he just sits there asking for help. And you might help now and then, but not indefinitely, because you know it's easy for the kid to get up and keep riding. So, you'd rather not intervene in this case, because you'd make the kid believe he can't do it on his own. As ridiculous as this analogy might sound to you, healing all of our planetary problems is much easier than we suspect. All that is required is a little more openness, transparency and success-mindedness coupled with love.

Within only a few years, all poverty can be eradicated and all war can come to a halt. Without needing to change political systems or force people to think or do this or that. Do you realize that, at a higher consciousness, it doesn't matter which political system is in place? They all work. It's not about the system, it's about the consciousness of the people using it. You have people fighting over various ideologies as if they made any difference. It doesn't matter whether you are sitting on the left or right side of the train. What matters is the quality of the people in the train, where the train is going and who built the tracks.

It is not wise for us to rely on outside intercessors to come and save us. Most of the beings in the vicinity of our solar system have the view that we are ourselves *responsible* for raising our own consciousness. There are too many books and websites that imply that we get help from aliens, and yet it really is our own job, not the job of some race on a distant planet. Speaking in analogy again, you might be willing to travel to that ancient tribe and lend a humanitarian hand, but it is ultimately up to them what they make of it. Moreover, your supposed help may have unintended consequences that are disruptive of their cohesion and culture. Why provide them with your smartphone when they are happier without? Perhaps they have telepathic abilities and do not need a smartphone to communicate over long distance.

To make the point even clearer: You love your pet cat and feed her and protect her as you can. But when she wanders off on her own adventures, you can hardly take responsibility for her jumping around on train tracks. It's up to her to learn to avoid them. We do have support from above, but we are meant to ascend out of our own power. That is, in fact, the whole *point* of our stay on Earth.

The Universe is not that much unlike our world, where you find the good, the bad, the ugly, the beautiful. You'll find the enlightened, who are rare, and those who pose as enlightened, who are many. You'll find the free and the slave. The rich and the poor. The good rich and the bad rich, the good poor and the bad poor and everything in between. Most people are actually in between. Pure negative and pure positive are rare. These two rare types of people are the ones who rule the world. Most people that appear to be negative or evil, are not. They are merely afraid and can be healed and forgiven. Those rare purely negative people that seem to be beyond repair and the purely positive people that are beyond anger, are so because they are aligned with various non-terrestrial energies, philosophies or groups.

Each and every variation that can exist, does exist. Anything you can imagine exists one some level, *otherwise you couldn't imagine it.* We've been misinformed on what imagination actually is — a method to derive information from other realms and levels. Our mind-based education system by passes the larger context of our reality. The fact that our scientific and religious institutions do not train us on the nature of reality is what makes books like these so much fun to read.

The eyes with which we view reality only perceive a tiny percentage of it. Imagine being a fish. You are living in water and do not clearly see the reality above water. Sometimes you see vague outlines of things moving above water. You hear garbled sounds and see what looks like shadows, moving. There are rumors of sentient *beings* living up there, but it's not easy for you to discern "who's who", and much of the speculation on it is inaccurate. The fish have many philosophers, speculating on what might be up there. The fish that found out that some of these beings use fish as food, is labeled a fear-monger. Even in the rare cases where one of these humans jumps right into the water, most are so terrified that they don't hang around to study these "aliens".

Our view of the Universe is similarly vague. Many of us intuitively or through experience know that "something else out there" exists, but not much else. Are the fish "kept in darkness" by malevolent intention or is it simply their nature and evolutionary level to be in the water and not clearly be able to see what is outside of it? In some areas there may be a secret intention to keep them there so that they serve merely as food, but largely, it is mostly their *nature* that prevents them from seeing higher. Interestingly, those that want to know more about life above water come closer to the shore. And they are also the ones most likely to be caught by fishermen.

This analogy is not as far-fetched as you might hope. In ancient Atlantis there was a cult that believed that, in order to rise above humanity and join their alien overlords, they'd have to see human beings. In those days, eating human flesh was viewed as a sign of royalty. Why? Because if one would eat human flesh they'd be considered "above humans" on the food chain. That is in fact one of the "cultural customs" that led to the Earth being destroyed by floods. The truth, of course, is that "eating humans" only leads to superiority if one does not believe in the spiritual nature of beings but rather in the "might is right" philosophy that is today known as Social Darwinism. Spiritual power is not gained from killing fellow humans, drinking their blood and eating their flesh, as these deluded ancients believed, it is gained through deriving spiritual energy from your inner components of emotion, imagination, attention and will.

Some of you may be wondering what that says about vegetarianism vs. eating animals. What it says is that the more we ascend in consciousness levels, the less we will have to eat. At this point in our evolution, animal meat gives our bodies strength and endurance, so I wouldn't necessarily call it harmful to eat meat (at reasonable quantities). I, myself, am not a vegetarian, but it is entirely clear to me that as we evolve to higher levels, we will eventually lose interest and lose the need for eating animals. At our final stage, we will give up eating altogether and derive sustenance from Light.

I have already gone into detail on the overall nature of reality in my other publications, but allow me to present this image as a brief recap:

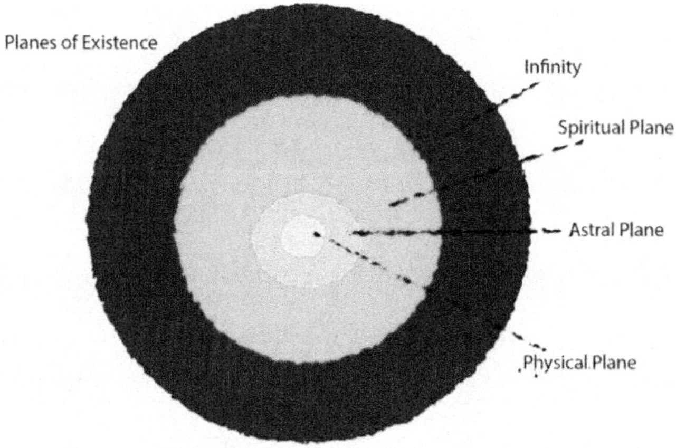

You can find a more detailed overview of the "Planes of Existence" in my video titled, "The Nature of Infinity", available for free online.

Discerning Astral, Extraterrestrial and Spiritual

Some beings exist simultaneously on the physical plane, the astral plane and the spiritual plane. Humans exist on all three planes, but are "normally" only aware of their existence on the physical plane. Some beings exist only in the astral and the physical. They are in a sense "soulless" because they have no existence or only very rudimentary fragments on the spiritual plane. We experience them as negative or outright evil, because they have "lost access" to their higher selves. Some beings exist on the physical and spiritual planes. These would mostly be considered positive. And then there those who exist primarily on the spiritual plane. They are composed of love and extreme amounts of energy and flow that love toward all beings. However, that still doesn't mean they are going to come here and save the day. If there is any intervention at all, it is usually only when they are called upon by humans themselves.

Humans have used the technique of prayer to call upon higher realm beings. So why are some prayers answered and some appear not to be? Well, actually *all* prayers are answered. If they appear not to be, it's because they are answered at another time than we wish they were.

One of the greatest misunderstandings of our time, in this kindergarten we call Earth, is that the entities that reside on the astral plane are "extraterrestrials". Many of them are not. Some of them only pose as ETs, some of them are mistaken for ETs. I guess in the original sense of the word, these astral beings are "aliens", but not so in the contemporary sense of physical beings coming from another planet to visit and explore. Most of these entities don't even have physical bodies. Rather than calling all of them extraterrestrial, it would be better to call them interdimensional. I'm sorry to say, but just this little piece of information, puts me at odds with 80% of the "UFO literature" out there. This "UFO literature" looks only at nuts-and-bolts explanations, yet not a single nut or bolt belonging to an extraterrestrial has been publicly presented. And yet, we have hundreds of thousands of people who have subjectively experienced UFOs and "aliens". I'm going to have to expound on this because it's a widely held misconception.

There are only very few UFOlogists who researched deeply enough to acknowledge the interdimensional quality of some of the UFOs and "ETs". One of them was the researcher Jacques Vallee. From his Wikipedia entry:

Jacques Fabrice Vallée (French: [vale]; born September 24, 1939) is a computer scientist, venture capitalist, author, ufologist and former astronomer currently residing in San Francisco, California.

In mainstream science, Vallée co-developed the first computerized map of Mars for NASA in 1963. He later worked on the network information center for the ARPANET, a precursor to the modern Internet, as a staff member of SRI International's Augmentation Research Center under Douglas Engelbart.

Vallée is also an important figure in the study of unidentified flying objects (UFOs), first noted for a defense of the scientific legitimacy of the extraterrestrial hypothesis and later for promoting the interdimensional hypothesis.

Vallée proposes that there is a genuine UFO phenomenon, partly associated with a form of non-human consciousness that manipulates space and time. The phenomenon has been active throughout human history, and seems to masquerade in various forms to different cultures. In his opinion, the intelligence behind the phenomenon attempts social manipulation by using deception on the humans with whom they interact.

Vallée also proposes that a secondary aspect of the UFO phenomenon involves human manipulation by humans. Witnesses of UFO phenomena undergo a manipulative and staged spectacle, meant to alter their belief system, and eventually, influence human society by suggesting alien intervention from outer space. The ultimate motivation for this deception is probably a projected major change of human society, the breaking down of old belief systems and the implementation of new ones. Vallée states that the evidence, if carefully analyzed, suggests an underlying plan for the deception of mankind by means of unknown, highly advanced methods. Vallée states that it is highly unlikely that governments actually conceal alien evidence, as the popular myth suggests. Rather, it is much more likely that that is exactly what the manipulators want us to believe. Vallée feels the entire subject of UFOs is mystified by charlatans and science fiction. He advocates a stronger and more serious involvement of science in the UFO research and debate.[10] Only this can reveal the true nature of the UFO phenomenon.

I quote Vallee's viewpoint because it aligns with what I have discovered independently while having out-of-body experiences. Out-of-body experiences allow a researcher to gain a wider perspective about how things work. I fully agree with Vallee's hypothesis about *deceptive intent* by interdimensional beings in conjunction with charlatans and possibly even government spooks. But even without out-of-body experiences, anyone with intelligence who has read a few UFO books will come to similar conclusions.

It is worth noting that Vallee is not just some kook, but was involved in the invention and creation of the internet for U.S. military intelligence. It is a little-known fact that a lot of well-known and bestselling UFO authors have close ties to U.S. intelligence and defense agencies. Whether that is a good thing or not, I don't know. What I do know is that the idea that many of these authors are people "on the fringes of society" is false. In "popular culture" (a Hollywood-created illusion), there is the idea that UFOlogists are fat kids or skinny nerds sitting in their mom's basement, when, in fact, they are more likely to be wearing suits and working for the CIA.

Most astral beings are purely non-physical. Some can manifest physically or appear to manifest physically but mostly they can only be perceived in an altered state of consciousness or when you have left your own body. By the way: If you had the ability to *leave your body consciously*, then you would be familiar with most of the information in this book rather than it sounding "far out".

A good example of mistaking astrals as ETS are the so-called "greys" which have been glorified as "space visitors" of "superior intelligence" in UFO literature and a seemingly endless series of movies and television shows. There are thousands of books on them. They first gained worldwide notoriety in the 1987 bestselling book *Communion* and follow-up books by Whitley Strieber.

The greys are seen as the beings piloting the flying saucers.

What is not well known is that Strieber himself sowed doubt in this "alien abduction" idea, decades after popularizing it. In recent years, he has revealed in public interviews that he thought the CIA had tampered with his mind, and that he had been subject to secret experimentation in their laboratories. He also revealed that he now thinks that there is something "very sinister" about the "grey aliens". After years of advocating for them, how's that for putting the whole thing into a bad light? The problem is that his books were published far and wide but his recantations received no such publicity. So even today, his books are still widely cited to support the "alien abduction" idea.

To me, the entire mythology around the "greys" is inaccurate. The greys are, in reality, entities of the lower astral realm. Moreover, according to my research and personal experience, most of the UFOs people witness in the sky are also not ETs, they are experimental, misinterpreted or secret government aircraft. Some of them are created and owned by supranational organizations that the public is blissfully unaware of.

One of the hints that the "greys" are lower astral entities is in the way they appear to people who receive their "visitations" and supposed "close encounters of the third kind": on the verge of sleep, fully asleep or in a state of trance. Another clue that they are *lower* astral, meaning non-friendly, is that they *impose* their presence and will upon humans. Any entity that *forces* itself into your presence, evoking fear and terror, cannot be said to be benevolent. Many of the books on "alien abduction" try to write this off as them being "just different than us" or "misunderstood" and that's why they impose. But non-imposition is a universal law of positive beings in the Universe. This is precisely why the Blue Beings that visited me, told me it was illegal for them to *directly* interact with me, much less without my consent. The greys are known for abducting people against their will and performing all sorts of experiments on them. That's not something a highly advanced alien race would do.

Some of these so-called “alien abduction” experiences are memory masks for sexual abuse events, which may or may not actually involve the greys. This is evidenced by the fact that throughout the literature on so-called “alien abductions”, there is a lot of “experimentation” on the sexual organs. In internet forums, it is common for people to joke about the “anal probing” of these supposed extraterrestrials.

With starry eyes, many wholeheartedly buy into the myth of the “grey ET” and would be disappointed to find that the whole thing is somewhat of a scam. That’s why it’s important to reiterate that there are indeed real ETs out there. In this Universe alone, there are trillions of lifeforms. All I am saying here is that some of these beings that *pose* as extraterrestrials are actually astral beings that have been toying with and tricking humans for thousands of years. Shamans knew them as nature spirits, sky spirits, water spirits. Christians knew them as demons. Muslims knew them as Jinn. They have taken on many shapes and forms throughout history, but in the end, they are simply lower astral beings. And the lower-astral realm is simply a belt of energy in and around Earth that is of lower spiritual density. It is populated by disconnected souls, some of which plot to influence humanity negatively. They have been allowed to do so because Earth is a training ground to awaken souls in spite of such challenges.

This is why people ridicule the UFO crowd. Because they intuitively sense the scam. But they mostly don't know that there are very real agendas behind it. Laughing them off with "extraterrestrials don't exist" is just as ignorant as embracing all these "aliens" as our space brothers and sisters.

The reason real ETs do not generally appear on Earth is because there is a galaxy-wide non-intervention treaty for our planet (apart from the unflattering fact that many alien races are just not that interested in us). The purpose of the non-intervention principle is so that human beings can grow and *find enlightenment on their own accord*, in their own time and of their own free will. Earth is a free will planet where the law and rule is that you can only experience something if you give your consent or permission. That law contradicts the idea of aliens intervening or imposing. ETs that do intervene, do so illegally. That means it is *possible* to undermine your free will if you are unconscious enough to allow for that. You are able to choose to have others choose for you.

The other main "ET" race that is mischaracterized, are the already-mentioned Reptilians. Ideas about them have become so widespread that they are regularly mentioned in pop culture. Here is David Ickes Wikipedia entry:

At the heart of Icke's theories lies the idea that that the universe is made up of "vibrational" energy, and consists of an infinite number of dimensions that share the same space. He believes that an inter-dimensional race of reptilian beings called the Archons (or Anunnaki), have hijacked the Earth, and that a genetically modified human/Archon hybrid race of shape-shifting reptilians, also known as the "Babylonian Brotherhood", the

Illuminati, or the 'elite', manipulate global events to keep humans in a constant state of fear, so the Archons can feed off the 'negative energy' this creates. He claims many prominent figures belong to the Babylonian Brotherhood, and are propelling humanity towards an Orwellian global fascist state, or New World Order; a post-truth era where freedom of speech is ended. Icke believes that the only way this 'Archontic' influence can be defeated is by humanity waking up to 'the truth', and filling their hearts with love.

Icke is correct that the universe is made up of vibrational energy and that freedom from oppression follows love. In that case, he should write more stuff on love. The "Archons" idea is also correct or semi-correct. The term "Archon" comes from "Gnosticism", an ancient philosophy that posits the God that created the Earth is an imposter-God that stands between us and a transcendent God. This transcendent God can only be reached through gnosis or enlightenment. So here we have the ultimate conspiracy theory and the root of most modern conspiracy theories. But from what I know, this core Gnostic idea of a cosmic conspiracy is not true. This galaxy, solar system and the Earth were created by benevolent beings for the purpose of growth. They were not created by malevolent Archons for the purpose of imprisonment. But in order to know that for sure, you have to ascend in consciousness levels. Otherwise the Gnostic belief could make sense to you.

What else is true is that we are not heading toward a global fascist state or "New World Order", we are actually heading toward greater levels of consciousness. In other words, the "bad guys" are not winning. They'd like to, but their tragedy is that no matter what they try to enslave humanity, they always lose in the end. How do I know this? Anyone familiar with history knows that there have always been villains aiming to "control the world" and "enslave humanity", always trying old schemes dressed in new clothes. Have they achieved it? No. You can fool some of the people some of the time but you can't fool all of the people all of the time.

According to David Icke and similar authors, most politicians and celebrities are "Reptilians" in human disguise. There are countless cheesy YouTube videos which purport to show politicians "shapeshifting" into lizards. I can't confirm *any* of that to be true in the slightest. The reason people come up with these fantastical ideas is because they sense there is something going on in the shadows but they don't quite know what. So, they project their imagination to fill in the gaps of what they don't know.

What I can confirm, is that the Serpent race has been in and around Earth for hundreds of thousands of years. Books by David Icke are merely the latest manifestation of reports on them. The ideas of "Archons" have been around for thousands of years. Here is a more detailed rundown of the Gnostic ideas from Wikipedia:

Gnosticism (from Ancient Greek: γνωστικός *gnostikos, "having knowledge", from* γνῶσις *gnōsis, knowledge) is a modern name for a variety of ancient religious ideas and systems, originating in Jewish-*

Christian milieus in the first and second century AD. These systems believed that the material world is created by an emanation of the highest God, trapping the divine spark within the human body. This divine spark could be liberated by gnosis. Some of the core teachings include the following:

All matter is evil, and the non-material, spirit-realm is good.

There is an unknowable God, who gave rise to many lesser spirit beings called Aeons.

One evil, lower spirit being is the creator who made the universe.

Gnosticism does not deal with 'sin', only ignorance. To achieve salvation, one needs to get in touch with secret knowledge.

The Syrian–Egyptian traditions postulate a remote, supreme Godhead, the Monad. From this highest divinity emanate lower divine beings, known as Aeons. The Demiurge, one of those Aeons, creates the physical world. Divine elements "fall" into the material realm, and are locked within human beings. This divine element returns to the divine realm when Gnosis, esoteric or intuitive knowledge of the divine element within, is obtained.

Those referred to as "Archons" in Gnosticism, are the same beings we today refer to as "Reptilians". Because they are so secretive and elusive, it's easy to get caught up in exaggerations about them. These authors intuitively feel their presence inside Earth. It's not that these are wrong or that Gnosticism does not have its merits. What's wrong is their *emphasis* on these creatures. These beings are not all-powerful. They do not enter the skin of politicians and celebrities or pose as humans. Their influence is more astral than physical. And no, in my view, they did not create this Universe and did not create Planet Earth. For thousands of years, the Serpent claims to be the Creator, but they are more imposters than creators.

I see it as my main responsibility as an author to bring more clarity into a confusing mix of paranormal and philosophical literature and this is one of the distinctions I've always wanted to make. People have written to me, telling me "You should read about Gnosticism, you'd love it" and I would think "Hmmm…not really". The fruits of Gnosticism: being suspicious about life itself.

These Archons or Reptilians, while real, shouldn't be the focus of humanity, apart from learning a little about their existence. There is so much more good than bad out there, and to write books showing mostly the bad, is a *distortion* of reality. It's as if I were to film a travel documentary about the U.S. showing only crime gangs, and at the end of the film, saying "Love is the Answer".

Yes, it's interesting and important to know that crime gangs exist in America. It's even of value to know where they are and how they might be overcome. But crime gangs are not the only things that exist in the U.S. and not even the "all powerful" force there. So what some of these researchers do is focus the lens on the worst of the worst, and blow their power and influence out of proportion, finally leaving you with the idea that all hope is lost. But if "love is the answer", then why not dedicate at least half of your research to the good, the true and the beautiful? This kind of writing is sensationalist because it appeals to human's desire for action and horror. You may think that the stuff I am writing in this book is just as "far out" and "bizarre", but in reality, I am writing from a perspective of matter-of-fact reporting, with no desire to embellish or warn. The reality I live in is of peace and tranquility with not a single threat far and wide, from the comfort of my couch, well fed, sipping self-made fruit juice and coffee and chewing on nuts.

I once visited a David Icke lecture that had to be cancelled midway because the author was continually coughing and spitting blood. Why might that be? He might say "because the Reptilians are psychically manipulating me". But *they don't have that power* over conscious and fearless individuals. Just like voodoo has no power over people who don't believe in it. In my view, he was falling ill from speaking, because 95% of his speaking was negatively focused. What you focus on all the time, does *affect* you.

That said, and for the sake of accuracy: Some of the reptilian species are capable of manifesting physically and some are born in the physical Universe. But they were more physical in pre-flood times, more than 12,000 years ago. After the flood, their primary domain became the astral realm, which is a counterfeit spiritual realm. As "fallen angels" they have lost access to the spiritual realm.

In their physical form, they mostly populate the inside of the Earth and Mars, where they are in hiding. They attempt to influence humanity negatively, through psychic and astral means. And why do I believe this is not really a problem for you personally? Because you are a human being. As such you have access to the spiritual realm, which is millions of grades stronger than their astral realm. Were you to use only a *tiny portion* of your power, they'd be long gone. In fact, the more people awaken to their power, the more uncomfortable their situation inside Earth gets. If they don't find some way to oppress humanity, they'll have to leave the planet. And their leaving the planet will lead to our spiritual ascension. It's like the relief you feel when getting rid of bad company, but on a worldwide scale.

The astral realms are mostly populated by negative beings. Some of them are energetically neutral. Some of them are moderately positive and playful. Many of them have good sides and bad sides, just like humans. But those in the lower astral realms are generally ill-intended and operate on fear, violence and slavery-based hierarchical systems. Why? Because the physical and astral universe operate on contrast and polarity, and also because these beings have a history of negativity, through their own choices.

These beings are certainly not superior, much less the providers of arcane knowledge or the saviors of humankind. Yes, they have provided us with a lot of secret knowledge throughout the ages but that always came with strings attached. They are able to divulge secrets that would make any recipient rich overnight, but not without a pay-off. This is the origin of the old archetype of "selling one's soul to the devil". Their knowledge is due to them being around for hundreds of thousands of years and the lack of restraints on their astral perception.

The lower astral realm is dense and unpleasant. It's the stuff of nightmares. Here, energy is always gained at the *expense* of others. These entities feed off of human hate, grief, shame and fear. The good news is that if you keep your own energy level moderately stable, you never have anything to do with these creatures. There are a lot of horror movies and ideas about demonic possession, etc., which make it look as if it's fairly easy to descend to those levels. But it's not. It takes a lot of fear and desolation over many years to even get that low. In our times, the consciousness level of the planet has increased to a level, where such evil is becoming increasingly rare and unpopular. The following table shows how energy is gained at the different levels.

How Energy is Gained at Different Consciousness Levels

Parasitic, Vampiric	At the lowest levels of consciousness, energy is gained 100% externally and at the exploitative, forcing and violent expense of others.
Drugs, Fear, Rage	At a low level of consciousness, energy is gained mostly externally through drugs and inciting negative emotions in self and others.
Foods, Oxygen, Attention	At a normal level of consciousness, energy is gained partially externally through foods, oxygen, water, sleep and the attention of other humans.
Mental Images, Communication, Motion	At a higher level of consciousness, energy is gained partially internally through ones own thoughts, exchange with others as well as through physical motion.
Love, Care, Creative Work	At a high level of consciousness, energy is gained largely internally through loving emotions, nurture and creative work.
From Within, Universe, Source	At the highest levels of consciousness, energy is not "gained", it is ever present as one is part of the overall infinite field. All energy is derived "internally", without dependence.

Published 2017 by
www.realitycreation.org

Having clarified the difference between astral and extraterrestrial, lets now talk about some actual ETs. You can tell actual ETs in what they look, feel and sound like. If they are more advanced than humans, they will actually look, sound and feel the part. They will look good! I have published sample pictures of them in the video that introduced this book (with the same title as this chapter) some time ago. These will not impose on you, they will not show up at night looking creepy and doing weird experiments on you. They will radiate the qualities we have always and will always associate with goodness: humor, peace, love, kindness, calm and wisdom. If they ever do enter your space, then it is by your permission. They might communicate with you through dreams, lucid dreams or telepathy, but they normally won't request to enter your physical body as in some channelings and mediumships. There is no reason whatsoever to have your body taken over by entities. Their ulterior reason for trying to enter your body is because they wish to experience physical reality, which is vibrationally above the lower astral. Beings of the celestial realms would never request that, not only because they do not impose but because the experience would be intensely unpleasant to them, not to mention an overwhelm to your own body.

Most of an ETs communication with you would be *telepathic*. Within my Pleiadean experience, I had to allow them to proceed before they opened communication. This is similar to a person first knocking on your door before they enter your house. Malevolent beings don't knock, they just enter. This is comparable to burglars who do not really care about your space, only about breaking, entering and taking whatever they can get.

So yes, you can contact and communicate with extraterrestrials, but it's fairly rare for Earthlings. You do not need ETs, angels or entities for your individual evolution. Such ideas are typical symptoms of a humanity that have lost confidence in their own power. That's why, for the past thirty years, I have been teaching "reality creation": to reduce dependence on external sources. You may have noticed that the most *enlightened beings* among humankind are independent. They are no one's employee. Many gurus advocate making use of non-physical beings, but I'd like you to know with certainty that you have all the knowledge, wisdom and love within, from *your Self that resides on the spiritual plane.* There is a version of you already residing on the higher plane, called your soul or essence and there is a version of you already residing on the astral plane called your "double" or astral self.

You are able to create your own reality to a large extent. You have been *grossly underestimating yourself* and in calling for the help of aliens, you assume they can do something for you that you cannot. Once you understand just who you are, it will become much easier to communicate with higher beings because you no longer show up as a beggar but as their equal. The only Source worth asking for guidance from, is the Highest Source in the Universe, the Ultimate Origin and Creator. You are a miniature version of the Highest Source and have the ability to access an infinite field of consciousness and energy, *within.*

And what does it mean when I and all these other teachers say "within"? Where is that? You find it when you close your eyes. With eyes closed, what you feel and sense is both your own energy and any foreign energy that might be around. The practice of meditators and energy workers is to get rid of foreign energy so that only your inherent energy is left in the end.

Some are curious about whether there are aliens disguised as humans on Earth. Do they "walk among us"? That's a fascinating subject. My answer to that is that anything is possible. If they are among us, I have no conscious awareness of it. I have met and seen people that looked oddly "out of place".

I once went hiking in an area that was devoid of civilization for a thousand miles in every direction when I saw a man in a suit and tie walking around the dense forest. My map indicated that the next small town would be seven hours away, the next highway perhaps eight hours distant and the next city maybe a twelve-hour drive. So, what exactly was a man in a suit doing wandering around these parts? I tried to follow where he was going but quickly lost sight of him. Reaching the point where I saw him there was nothing but shrubs, bushes and trees. In fact, there wasn't even a path. That's an example of an incident that struck me as a possible "alien encounter". Unless perhaps he was part of a film shoot. Or maybe there was some secret underground base nearby and he had surfaced for some reason.

The beautiful thing is that there is much more happening than our wildest imagination could ever conceive of. You might wonder what I was doing at such a remote place. I sometimes take walks and hikes in remote areas to increase my intuition away from chatter, electronic frequencies from cell phone towers and the chatter of other people's thoughts. Yes, people's thoughts are a form of chatter that can be sensed. If you don't believe this, take a walk at 5 a.m. before the chattering minds of people wake up. You'll feel the difference.

The spiritual plane is populated by beings of higher consciousness, some of which we call angels. I have written about these higher beings extensively in my book *Lives of the Soul.* Many people assume that they are talking to or channeling "angels" or what they call "guardian angels" and "ascended masters". This is yet another misunderstanding I'd like to clear up. The energy vibration of the spiritual realms is so powerful that your nervous system couldn't handle it. Your spirit can handle it, but not the body. For this reason, enlightened beings generally don't communicate *directly* with humans. If anything, they communicate with your Higher Self (soul) and your Higher Self may or may not relay that information down to "you" (the mind) in the form of dreams and synchronicities.

So, if there is a channeled entity calling itself an "angel", it probably isn't. It's instead a being from the higher astral realm, the mid astral realm or the lower astral realm. And this being that you are talking to or that is talking through you, may or may not be benevolent. Likewise, when you are taking drugs such as Ayahuasca or DMT, the entities you see, no matter how magnificent they seem to you, are always astral. These drugs allow for viewing of the astral, they never allow for viewing of the spiritual. Of course, there are hundreds of drug-experiencers who write entire books on their "spiritual experience" without the slightest inkling that there is a much higher realm.

The undeveloped body does not have the capacity to view the spiritual plane. There are ways to prepare the body for higher states of consciousness (such as fasting, meditation, prayer and advanced yoga), but in general, your viewing of the spiritual plane is limited to certain lucid dreams, out-of-body experiences and singular high-state events. People who use the drug DMT are especially prone to believing they had a "spiritual experience". DMT opens the gates of perception to a particular area of the astral realm. They report seeing robotic elves, strange super-advanced gadgets and spinning, circling, oscillating geometric figures. And as amazing as all of that is, it's still the astral realm.

The extremely powerful, bright, shining beings of the spiritual realm sometimes intervene in the form of miracles and synchronicity. In rare cases they might prevent accidents or appear as visionary dreams or send hunches. But they rarely talk to you directly, much less appear, unless you yourself are at an extraordinarily high state of a saint or sage.

The Pleiadeans who contacted me used a form of telepathy. For this they first had to manipulate frequencies around me — I felt an odd shifting sensation at the center of my brain. I do not know how common or rare this kind of telepathy is. For me, it is obviously rare.

How do I know that these Pleiadeans were not the astral-level tricksters I keep talking about? Well, the astral realm is a very distinct quality that is easily recognizable once you get used to it. At a younger age I took frequent out-of-body travels in the astral realm. I know what it feels like, sounds like, looks like. It's like an expert in food could *easily* tell the difference between freshly cooked and previously frozen food. Study creates familiarity and familiarity creates expertise. The astral realms have an underlying sadness to them. At the lower astral this sadness is suffocating. At the higher astral, its masked through all kinds of pretty colors and glitter (such as that seen on DMT). My encounter with the extraterrestrials, on the other hand, had a realism to them that is not found with the astral.

When a so-called deceased relative is talking to you, it's not your deceased relative but yet another *entity* posing as such. Why? Because deceased people will usually linger for a few minutes, hours or three days at the very most, before they move on or ascend. The realms of the afterlife are distant, relatively speaking, so their communication with you on Earth is unlikely. You might believe they have something important to tell you, but when a spirit leaves the body, many of the earthly urgencies are seen as illusory and there are vastly more *real* things to attend to. If they were actually able to talk to you through some medium, that wouldn't be a good sign because it means they are stuck in the astral realm. So, it's not your grandmother talking, but an astral trickster entity. The reason they know so much, including private information about yourself, is not because they are your grandma, but because they are not bound by physical limitations.

Psychic abilities are no proof of higher consciousness, and this "deep arcane knowledge" does not make them superior to you. I, too, have psychic abilities, but that doesn't mean I'm enlightened, it merely means I'm able to switch off my mind. You, too, have these abilities. Indicators of a being (human or otherwise) having a higher level of consciousness are not psychic abilities or psychedelic altered states, but an easy-going nature, loving kindness, humility, humor, integrity and undivided presence.

As I've written before, there are altered states and higher states. Altered states are encounters with the astral, higher states are encounters with the spiritual. Contrary to the recommendations of 90% of self-improvement teachers, I do not advise soliciting the help of aliens, entities or angels. But if you do so anyway, then *at least* make sure you are focusing on the most beautiful that you can imagine. You will always attract those physical and non-physical beings that you resonate with. It's fairly easy to attract anything into your life, merely by sustained focus. If you use prayer, I don't recommend you pray to angels, but rather only to the Highest Source, by which angels may or may not be deployed.

If you are into lucid dreaming, know this: Lucid dreaming is travelling in the lower astral, mid astral and higher astral realms. In rare cases, lucid dreams transport you into the spiritual planes. In lucid dreams you can casually meet all kinds of beings as your non-physical self. Whether this is a good or bad experience, largely depends upon what *you* radiate. Just keep in mind that positive beings will be very clear on who they are, they will not ask anything from you or try to impose on you or cut deals or require some pay off from you. You won't have to sacrifice a goat to gain their favor. They will remind you of your inherent abilities and show you the sheer beauty of the Universe. All else is just another variation of the victim and neediness program that humans have been running for thousands of years.

Transhumanism vs. Spirituality

Within the physical realm there are various densities of physicality. Steam is less dense than water. Water is less dense than ice. Ice is less dense than mud. And mud is less dense than metal.

On our planet, we are currently in a phase where we want to merge humans with artificial intelligence. We are trying to create a hybrid or android by merging the physical body with electronics and metal parts. We call this Transhumanism. Proponents of Transhumanism claim that this is the next step in the evolution of humankind. But this kind of *incarnation into virtual reality*, is not actually an ascent of consciousness, as widely claimed, but a deeper *descent* into the physical plane. Our merging with computers and robots would actually subvert humans free will and further our ignorance of our inherent spiritual powers.

This has already happened to some extent in that our electronic devices have replaced and supplanted spiritual abilities. For example, Google Maps has replaced our spiritual sense of spatial orientation. Search engines have replaced intuitive asking and intuitive knowing. The focus of will and intention is replaced by receiving images from screens. It may therefore come as a surprise to readers, that I cannot wholeheartedly support Transhumanism as I am aware of the spiritual self. Nor do I seek "life extension" in the body because I know I am not the body and never was. After my physical body dies, I wish to ascend to the next level of the game. If we are not the body, why is there a desire to prolong life in the body?

The body is nothing other than a temporary vehicle to experience a set of karmic lessons while on earth. These life extension and A.I. philosophies make no mention of the spirit and that it's actually a good and desirable thing to pass away after a full life, and to move on. There are more much greater things that await us. The idea of extending life by merging with robots is borne out of materialistic-scientific atheism that could only be embraced by people who have forgotten their true nature and what their personal energy is truly capable of. Decades ago, I witnessed firsthand, the re-growth of an amputated arm through a group of healers. A robot's arm to replace the amputees, only becomes necessary because we have forgotten our ability to regrow it through focusing spiritual energy. In this way, we seek to replace lost power with technology. That's not to say that technology is "bad". It is an *extension* of who we are, not a replacement. The greatest danger of merging with robots is the loss of free will and further enslavement into the Illusion of physical reality as the "only" reality.

I am going to share something here that you may not have read and may never read anywhere else: In the coming age of robots and androids, you should know that when a human merges with metal, electricity and virtual reality, he is merging with a denser form of the physical world. Electricity is a variant of fire and originates in the astral realm. The physical body was created to be moderately dense, but it being full of the less dense water and blood, makes it lighter. As an android, it will be too dense to carry spiritual energy. It can then only feed off astral energy (electricity) for sustenance. I therefore recommend that you do not replace body parts with machines. This warning may not make any sense right now, but it will, as techno-humans become more popular.

Your Astral Self

Before learning that there are physical, astral and spiritual versions of various aliens, perhaps I should have first told you about the non-physical versions of yourself. A lot has been written about your physical self (your body and mind) as well as your spiritual self (often called your Soul) but there is very little information out there on your astral self. The following paragraphs provide an introduction.

I recall a nightmare about moving into another house. The house looked strangely familiar but I didn't like it. Then I remembered that I had lived in this house before and was moving back into it. Why was I moving back into a house I had been so eager to leave? No, I had not lived here in real life, I had lived here in the dreamscape.

There is one type of dream in which you remember past dreams belonging to the same story. In fact, I remember an entire timeline and life, with recurring places and people, being lived on dreamscape. There was another dream on the same night. I was at a certain beach beside a sad looking, run-down hotel. Upon taking a swim, I suddenly remembered that I was in waters that were hard to get out of. "Wait! I'm making the same mistake again! I've been to this beach many times and know that the waters suck you in, so why am I swimming here again?"

Memory is very much dependent on the state you are in. Change your state, and your timeline and memory change. This is why certain timelines and dreams are only remembered when you happen to return to that specific frequency. Everything in the Universe is just different vibratory frequencies.

Over the years, I have learned that I have a *double in the dreamscape* — another version of me that is living out another life. While his thoughts and attitudes are similar to mine, he makes different choices leading to other realities. It took decades before I realized that this doppelgänger actually lives in what I call the astral realm, and that other people also have a double who lives in that realm. Some of the people I know in this life, I also know "on the other side". This doppelganger is not the same thing as "parallel universe versions of self" as described in my book, it is the astral self. Once I made the realization, I went to check what is commonly known about it. From Wikipedia:

A doppelgänger (literally "double-goer") is a look-alike or double of a living person, sometimes portrayed as a ghostly or paranormal phenomenon and usually seen as a harbinger of bad luck. Other traditions and stories equate a doppelgänger with an evil twin. In modern times, the term twin stranger is occasionally used. The word "doppelgänger" is often used in a more general and neutral sense to describe any person who physically or behaviorally resembles another person.

The doppelganger I refer to is something other than a lookalike. Ancient tradition referred to it as the "evil twin" because he/she lives in the astral realm, some parts of which have a nightmarish, super-negative vibe, as opposed to the higher spiritual realm. The part of me that is living in the spiritual realm is my soul or essence or Higher Self, which is different from this doppelganger. In summary: Everyone has a Higher Self and a lower self. The doppelganger appears to be a lower self, but even this lower self can heal, grow, learn and become more enlightened.

And this is what "science" has to say about it, again from Wikipedia:

Heautoscopy is a term used in psychiatry and neurology for the hallucination of "seeing one's own body at a distance". It can occur as a symptom in schizophrenia and epilepsy, and is considered a possible explanation for doppelgänger phenomena.

You can see why I sometimes put the word "science" in quotations. A science that explains every paranormal perception as a mental derangement or chemical imbalance, cannot be said to be a complete science. From the perspective of consciousness research, seeing the doppelganger in physical reality, comes from a rare overlap between the astral realm and the physical realm.

Schizophrenia may actually be the emergence of various astral entities (including, but not limited to, your doppelganger), inadvertently overlapping with yourself in physical reality. In any case, the entire field requires more research.

Some consciousness teachers say that what happens in dreams is the actual reality, whereas what happens in physical life is the dream. It is said that "life is just a dream" or an illusion. In some cases, people with this attitude reversal are living in the "mirror universe" (which is another word for astral realm, where the doppelganger has taken control of your consciousness. More specifically, our physical universe seen as "unreal" indicates either lower astral consciousness or higher spiritual consciousness. It is only from these vantage points that our physical life on earth seems unreal.

Mid-level consciousness experiences physical reality as real or substantial. In a low-vibe state, the world looks gray and vague while your adventures on astral plane look exciting. In a high-vibe state, our physical world looks comical and staged while the spiritual realm is deeper and fulfilling.

If you or another are saying "this world is not real", check whether that is coming from your lower self or your Higher Self. From a lower state, the unreal world is seen as bleak, dark, stupid, hopeless, ignorant and there is a tendency to develop hatred toward humans. From a higher state, the unreal world is seen as funny, cartoon-like and in-need-of-care. It's a simple formula: Hate comes from lower realms; Love comes from higher realms. Knowing just that is enough for discernment.

Which brings us back to our "evil twin" and his adventures in the dreamscape. The doppelganger represents the lost and split off part of yourself. My own "evil twin" is not actually evil. He just stumbles through the dreamscape puzzled and confused, repeating certain mistakes, but he is essentially a good guy. You will find your doppelganger at different levels of consciousness. The goal is not to become your doppelganger, but to heal him/her. In this sense, nightmares and confusing dreams are healing processes. Of course, not all of your dreams take you to the doppelganger reality. Some take you to your Higher Self. Some are garbled processing of subconscious material. Some dreams take you to other universes entirely. But the ones that have a nightmarish quality or indicate some sort of repetitive stuck-ness and recall of past dreams, usually refer to the mirror-life being lead on the astral plane. You can use these nightmares for healing through loving awareness. Just knowing about the lost/wandering nature of the doppelganger will, in time, help you lose the fear of nightmares. Fear is replaced with goodwill - your calm presence while witnessing his life, is all that is required for him/her to get better.

Reacting to nightmares with fear, attests to your ignorance of what is going on. It is not your essence experiencing, it is your double. The idea is to re-integrate this split off part of you through the universal and invincible power of appreciation. Once that process is complete, you are your "whole self" again and the quality of your dreams improves. Your dreams then take you to higher astral realms and possibly even spiritual realms and you will wake up in the morning recalling intensely beautiful experiences.

This then, is actually about a lighter approach to nightmares and the goal of maintaining awareness and calm throughout. If you have coached yourself to remain calm when trouble happens in waking life, you can do the same in sleeping life. Please note that if you do not experience any nightmares, you have already integrated split off aspects of self.

In summary of this chapter, we have come to classify the following beings and where they have a presence or "self":

	Physical Realm	Astral Realm	Spiritual Realm
Humans	yes	yes	yes
Most Extraterrestrials	yes	yes	yes
Entities such as Greys, Jinn, Demons, etc.	no	yes	no

Entities such as Reptilians	Yes	yes	no
Enlightened Beings	Sometimes	no	yes
Angels	no	no	yes

CHAPTER FIVE

THE SECRET HISTORY OF EARTH

The angelic beings have a presence in the spiritual realm, but not in the astral or physical. Because they occupy a higher context, they can influence the astral and physical, but they do not reside there. The ancient serpent has a home in the astral but no access to the spiritual plane. They have some influence on the physical realm, but are today more native to the astral. Put differently: Some of these fallen angels have fallen even deeper. In the ancient past, they were more present in physical form. Ancient Carvings from China, Sumeria, Mexico and South America show them using advanced aircraft, letting themselves be worshipped as gods and requesting human sacrifices for their favors. The Serpent is intimately linked to the history of Planet Earth and it is ultimately at their hand that human history is covered-up and erased. To introduce our hidden history, I will let another author, Michael Harner, speak for a few minutes. He has written one of the classics of New Age spiritual literature with the 1980 book, *The Way of the Shaman.*

In it, the author describes the history of humanity as revealed to him during his very first intake of Ayahuasca. While I personally don't recommend or use drugs, I am not saying that information derived from them is inaccurate. The following account, in fact, reveals one of the great hidden truths of our planet and very much aligns with my own research and experience:

Just a few minutes earlier I had been disappointed, sure that the ayahuasca was not going to have any effect on me. Now the sound of rushing water flooded my brain. My jaw began to feel numb, and the numbness was moving up to my temples. Overhead the faint lines became brighter, and gradually interlaced to form a canopy resembling a geometric mosaic of stained glass. The bright violet hues formed an ever-expanding roof above me. Within this celestial cavern, I heard the sound of water grow louder and I could see dim figures engaged in shadowy movements. As my eyes seemed to adjust to the gloom, the moving scene resolved itself into something resembling a huge fun house, a supernatural carnival of demons. In the center, presiding over the activities, and looking directly at me, was a gigantic, grinning crocodilian head, from whose cavernous jaws gushed a torrential flood of water. Slowly the waters rose, and so did the canopy above them, until the scene metamorphosed into a simple duality of blue sky above and sea gradually interlaced to form a canopy resembling a geometric mosaic of stained glass. All creatures had vanished. Then, from my position near the surface of the water, I began to see two strange boats wafting back and forth, floating through the air towards me, coming closer and closer. They slowly combined to form a single vessel with a huge dragon-headed prow, not unlike that of a Viking ship. Set amidships was a square sail. Gradually, as the boat gently floated back and forth above me, I heard a rhythmic swishing sound and saw that it was a giant galley with several hundred oars moving back and forth in cadence with the sound. I became conscious, too, of the most beautiful singing I have ever heard in my life, high-pitched and ethereal, emanating from myriad voices on board the galley. As I looked more closely at the deck, I could make out large numbers of people with the heads of blue jays and the bodies of humans, not unlike the bird-headed gods of ancient Egyptian tomb paintings. At the same time, some energy-essence began to float from my chest up into the boat. Although I believed myself to be an atheist, I was completely certain that I was dying and that the bird-headed people had come to take my soul away on the boat. While the soul-flow continued from my chest, I was aware that the extremities of my body were growing numb. Starting with my arms and legs, my body slowly began to feel like it was turning to solid concrete. I could not move or speak. Gradually, as the numbness closed in on my chest, toward my heart, I tried to get my mouth to ask for help, to ask the Indians for an antidote. Try as I might, however, I could not marshal my abilities sufficiently to make a word. Simultaneously, my abdomen seemed to be turning to stone, and I had to make a tremendous effort to keep my heart beating. I began to call my heart my friend, my dearest friend of all, to talk to it, to encourage it to beat with all the power remaining at my command. I became aware of my brain. I felt—physically—that it had become compartmentalized into four separate and distinct levels. At the uppermost surface was the observer and commander, which was conscious of the condition of my body, and was responsible for the attempt to keep my heart going. It perceived, but purely as a spectator, the visions emanating from what seemed to be the nether portions of my brain. Immediately below the topmost level I felt a numbed layer, which seemed to have been put out of commission by the drug—it just wasn't there. The next level down was the source of my visions, including the soul boat. Now I was virtually certain I was about to die.

As I tried to accept my fate, an even lower portion of my brain began to transmit more visions and information.

I was "told" that this new material was being presented to me because I was dying and therefore "safe" to receive these revelations. These were the secrets reserved for the dying and the dead, I was informed. I could only very dimly perceive the givers of these thoughts: giant reptilian creatures reposing sluggishly at the lowermost depths of the back of my brain, where it met the top of the spinal column. I could only vaguely see them in what seemed to be gloomy, dark depths. Then they projected a visual scene in front of me. First they showed me the planet Earth as it was eons ago, before there was any life on it. I saw an ocean, barren land, and a bright blue sky. Then black specks dropped from the sky by the hundreds and landed in front of me on the barren landscape. I could see that the "specks" were actually large, shiny, black creatures with stubby pterodactyl-like wings and huge whale-like bodies. Their heads were not visible to me. They flopped down, utterly exhausted from their trip, resting for eons. They explained to me in a kind of thought language that they were fleeing from something out in space. They had come to the planet Earth to escape their enemy. The creatures then showed me how they had created life on the planet in order to hide within the multitudinous forms and thus disguise their presence. Before me, the magnificence of plant and animal creation and speciation—hundreds of millions of years of activity—took place on a scale and with a vividness impossible to describe. I learned that the dragon-like creatures were thus inside of all forms of life, including man. They were the true masters of humanity and the entire planet, they told me. We humans were but the receptacles and servants of these creatures. For this reason they could speak to me from within myself. These revelations, welling up from the depths of my mind, alternated with visions of the floating galley, which had almost finished taking my soul on board. The boat with its blue-jay headed deck crew was gradually drawing away, pulling my life force along as it headed toward a large fjord flanked by barren, worn hills. I knew I had only a moment more to live. Strangely, I had no fear of the bird-headed people; they were welcome to have my soul if they could keep it. But I was afraid that somehow my soul might not remain on the horizontal plane of the fjord but might, through processes unknown but felt and dreaded, be acquired or re-acquired by the dragon-like denizens of the depths. I suddenly felt my distinctive humanness, the contrast between my species and the ancient reptilian ancestors. I began to struggle against returning to the ancient ones, who were beginning to feel increasingly alien and possibly evil.

Each heart beat was a major undertaking. I turned to human help. With an unimaginable last effort, I barely managed to utter one word to the Indians: "Medicine!" I saw them rushing around to make an antidote, and I knew they could not prepare it in time. I needed a guardian who could defeat dragons, and I frantically tried to conjure up a powerful being to protect me against the alien reptilian creatures. One appeared before me; and at that moment the Indians forced my mouth open and poured the antidote into me. Gradually, the dragons disappeared back into the lower depths; the soul boat and the fjord were no more. I relaxed with relief. The antidote radically eased my condition, but it did not prevent me from having many additional visions of a more superficial nature. These were manageable and enjoyable. I made fabulous journeys at will through distant regions, even out into the galaxy; created incredible architecture; and employed sardonically grinning demons to realize my fantasies. Often I found myself laughing aloud at the incongruities of my adventures. Finally, I slept.

And later in the book:

I was now eager to solicit a professional opinion from the most supernaturally knowledgeable of the Indians, a blind shaman who had made many excursions into the spirit world with the aid of the ayahuasca drink. It seemed only proper that a blind man might be able to be my guide to the world of darkness. I went to his hut, taking my notebook with me, and described my visions to him segment by segment. At first I told him only the highlights; thus, when I came to the dragon-like creatures, I skipped their arrival from space and only said, "There were these giant black animals, something like great bats, longer than the length of this house, who said that they were the true masters of the world." There is no word for dragon in Conibo, so "giant bat" was the closest I could come to describe what I had seen. He stared up toward me with his sightless eyes, and said with a grin, "Oh, they're always saying that. But they are only the Masters of Outer Darkness." He waved his hand casually toward the sky. I felt a chill along the lower part of my spine, for I had not yet told him that I had seen them, in my trance, coming from outer space.

I highlighted these sections of the book, decades ago, as a teenager. They caught my attention because I was able to fill in details while the author was recounting the story. I had seen similar scenes on my soul travels, as far back as childhood. I knew who these reptiles were escaping from, who they were in a galactic war with, why they were hiding on Earth and why they kept claiming they were the "Creators" of humankind and the "Masters of this World". Much of what I know about them, I have put into my books on Atlantis. Anyone who has read the Bible, the Quran, Ancient Chinese, Greek and Mayan mythology, the Vedas or any other number of writings on the ancient Gods and merely *contextualizes* these writings as tales of ancient inter-galactic and interstellar conflicts, clearly sees and knows what happened. The conflict goes back hundreds of thousands of years, according to Sumerian, Vedic and Egyptian timelines.

Once upon a time, pure consciousness manifested as units of energy or what we call souls. These spiritual beings *descended* in order to manifest as physical beings, for the purpose of exploring their creation. They created universes and then galaxies and decided to enter them as creatures rather than creators. *Entire universes were created as game-like activities.* Incarnating into them was seen like entering a virtual reality game. Eventually more challenging games were created and with that, suffering. Some beings forgot that they were playing a game, which only increased the suffering.

Take this as analogy or reality, as you prefer: Because the physical and astral realms are like smaller copies of the higher realms, the very same behaviors are happening now, as we develop virtual reality gaming. Gamers that get really good at their games, demand more challenging scenarios. So more difficult levels of gaming are introduced. Soon they become so difficult, they are almost impossible to escape from. And the gamers enjoy it because it strengthens their focus and determination. In other words, they enjoy becoming entrapped so that they can prove their skills of untangling themselves. This is precisely the motive that created this Universe and our situation in it. We are trapped in a system, we do not remember how we got here, how to get out and what is beyond it.

This game has a high level of difficulty. When this happens, we'd like to press the "emergency abort" button so that we can finally leave the game and ascend to our original position outside of it. Fortunately, we have such an emergency abort button. All that is required of us, is to make the highest source we can imagine, the main focus of our heart, to make a higher realm outside of the game our main priority. In doing so, we slowly gravitate upwards and eventually exit the game.

Another way to exit it is through natural death of your game-character (your body-mind). Your game is pre-programmed to have a "time's up" and when its time is expired, the game ends and your body-mind dies. Suicide doesn't work because it contradicts the previously programmed timing. Suicide means you'll end up neither here nor there, in an unpleasant limbo state that would require outside assistance to fish you out. So, you have free will within the game but you do not have free will over things you programmed into the game. The only way to regain free will over them is to go back to the position in which you made those choices.

The game called Earth has a set of pre-defined rules within which there is plenty of space for not yet defined free will choices. So, you can choose to focus on that which is outside of the game if you want to leave (or make the game easier) or you can simply wait until you naturally pass away. And it is for this reason that I don't support so called "life extension" – the only thing I'd be extending is my remaining in the game.

A part of the intergalactic war is a conflict going back hundreds of thousands of years between light and darkness. According to Buddhist and Hindu scripts, these "fallen gods" have merely descended in consciousness levels and can once again ascend. Some of the "bad guys" actually do ascend every now and then. They have successfully liberated themselves from a game they were trapped in. That is an incredible feat in gaming expertise. In this Universe, The Serpent represents one of the aspects of darkness. Their empire spreads throughout parts of our galaxy and other galaxies. It is a tiny faction of this race that is currently and secretly occupying Planet Earth. Their previous occupation was already once destroyed in the Great Flood approximately 12,000 years ago. About 6,000 years ago, they began infiltrating our planet again, this time covertly, as to stay undetected by their enemies.

Please re-read the last paragraph again to grasp the gravity of what I just said. But there is the one major point where conspiracy theorists are wrong: They believe that our secret rulers are overwhelmingly powerful, that we are mere cattle, that "everything is controlled" and that divulging this information can get you killed. They dismiss and block out all the "good guys" and also the pertinent fact that we have been winning this intergalactic war, always win in the end (by universal law, as the Universe is made from benevolence) and that not a single human being has to have anything to do with the dark Empire. Why? Because humans are connected to the spiritual Plane and the Serpent is not. So before sharing this information in detail, it was necessary for me to first educate on people's inherent inner power and ability to raise their vibration. Once a human being feels solid, strong, optimistic, loving, that human being cannot be harmed in any way, shape or form and can then be told what overall galactic situation they find themselves in.

Strictly speaking, the dark side is not entirely cut off from the spiritual realm. Nothing can be, because, seen from an even higher level, everything in this multiverse is ONE, derives from ONE source and will eventually return to that ONE source. And what happens in between, is simply the game.

How does one descend to the dark side? In this way: There are games one can enter that do not end with death. Some become entrapped in these games. And that's fun for a while, but over thousands of years it can become first frustrating and then agonizing and finally hopeless. When things become hopeless, a being yearns for annihilation. They develop the belief that through annihilation, their existence ends. But it doesn't. It just keeps repeating itself. And this is where ideas of "eternal damnation" and "Hell" come from. So, in order to achieve annihilation or what they call "liberation" (which never ends up in liberation), they attempt to commit acts that are in total defiance of Universal Laws. For example, you might be promised to be annihilated if you blow up an entire planet full of innocent people. You are told that if you commit such an atrocity, then surely your soul will be extinguished. But all that does is let you descend into further misery out of which is even more difficult to get out of. And that's the short version story of how people descend. It all starts with hardship and apathy. There is a 1992 movie called *Groundhog Day* which very aptly portrays both the problem and the solution. The main character of the movie, experiences the exact same undesirable day, over and over. He tries to escape it by committing all kinds of unlawful acts. When that doesn't work, he commits suicide. And when that doesn't work he begins developing genuine love and creativity by which he is finally liberated from the repetition loop.

This solar system was once populated on Mars and on another planet that exploded into what is now the asteroid belt. Some speculate that this planet was called "Phaeton". One day we will find a lot of interesting artefacts there, tucked away in asteroid rocks. Both planets hosted human societies that lived both on the surface and inside of these planets. I have no clear perception of what Phaeton looked like, but I was able to remote view ancient Mars. When the attackers arrived, they first destroyed communities and cities on the surface. Much of the population fled underground, where vast tunnel systems and cities had been built. I actually recall having lived there and dying from falling into one of Mars interior crevices after an explosion. In childhood, I had recurring dreams about that particular invasion and how I was holding my wife's hand, running for escape. She died from rocks falling on her head; I died from falling down the precipice. Mars had and still has incredibly large abysses, and people used to walk alongside them on a footway of red sand. Most of these walkways had railings, but this one didn't and I fell down it. I still sometimes feel that falling sensation and memory when I visit high places on Earth. Even though the memory must be at least a hundred thousand years old, it is still stored in my consciousness.

Beings from the spiritual plane — *The Creators* — formed those human-like civilizations on Mars and Phaeton. At one point, hundreds of thousands of years ago, the Serpent entered our solar system and destroyed those planets as part of an ongoing intergalactic war. Being mostly physical and having developed on this plane for hundreds of thousands of years, they had the technology to destroy entire planets. Some of the human-like beings on those planets fled the solar system and survived in other parts of the galaxy. I was not among those, I was among the ones who died there. These pre-Earth humans have records of a time the Earth didn't even exist yet. Nonetheless, if you read these historical records spanning hundreds of thousands of years, you wouldn't learn that many new things, because the dramas on the physical plane keep repeating themselves in many variations until the end of time.

Past-present-future are one and the same at a specific level of consciousness. Based on the past, one can predict the future. The faces and characters may change, but the core plot of the story stays the same, until there is a vibrational shift. What you do learn from studying history is patterns, and once you see the repeating patterns, you can transcend them.

The counter-force arrived on the scene a little too late, but when they did, they expelled the Serpent from this solar system. Why they arrived too late I don't know, but by the time they arrived, Phaeton had become the asteroid belt and Mars was being controlled by the Serpent race. The Creators didn't use physical technology to eradicate them. They used spiritual pulsed energy to get rid of them. I don't quite understand the procedure, but it's similar to using a frequency pulse device against rat infestation. Some of the reptile beings however, hid and nested deep within the interior of Mars.

The Creators proceeded to create Planet Earth. The intention was to make up for the destruction of Mars and Phaeton. Because they were present in both the spiritual and the physical, they had the extraordinary ability to design and populate entire worlds. The desire to create and populate worlds is not much different from our desire to create a home for our family, pet or, if we are city planners, our community. It was their sorrow for allowing that level of destruction and their love for humanity, that motivated the creation of Earth.

Religious readers among you will say, "But that contradicts the idea that God created Earth and the humans in seven days." To which I respond: I do not claim or aim to be aligned with the previously discussed veils (religion, science and New Age spirituality). However, none of this actually *contradicts* the world's great religions. In this example, the creation story is merely *transposed to a greater context.* I believe religious creation stories are *accurate*, but they are short-hand versions of what happened, told to an audience that wouldn't understand the details.

In a similar vein, "religious" people claim that the ancient alien theory contradicts the idea of a Creator God, because it claims we were created by aliens. But the idea of ancient aliens does not contradict the God idea, it merely transposes it. Even if we were created by aliens, who created the aliens? And who created those who created the aliens? Whichever way you put it, things always go back to an originating *Source*.

Our *Souls* were created by the Highest Source. This Highest Source is indescribable in human words, an Infinite Context. This Highest Source created beings that act in lower realms on its behalf. There is a Universal-Authority acting on behalf of the Highest Source. And there is a "Galactic Authority" that acts on the "Universal Authority". Seen from a higher perspective, the entire Universe with its entire history, was already set and determined from the very beginning. Yet to us, it *looks as if* it's a story playing out in time.

The beings that created the Earth and human bodies, were acting under the directive of the "Galactic Council". That Galactic Council reports directly to the Highest Source. The Highest Source is the origin of all things and universes. The Galactic Council are highly advanced beings of the spiritual realm, but they are not as advanced as the beings that oversee the entire Universe. And, strictly speaking, the authority of the entire Universe is still not "The Highest Source", because they are authority over only one Universe, not the Multiverse. But for the sake of brevity, it is ok to see the creator of this Universe and the Highest Source as equivalent.

In the biblical story of the Garden of Eden, it is said that God was walking around the Garden calling for Adam, who had eaten the forbidden fruit. The original Hebrew does not say it was "The Most High God" walking around the Garden of Eden, but rather a group of beings called *The Elohim.* The Elohim were actually representatives of the Galactic Council and it is they that created Earth and humans rather than the Most High Source of the Universe taking a stroll in a garden on Earth. So while not contradicting religious narrative, it is helpful to put these ancient stories into a wider global and even galactic framework.

Back in the early days of Earth, space travel to and from Earth was as casual as our airplane travel today. Our distant ancestors travelled far beyond our solar system, colonizing other parts of the galaxy. We have relatives all over the Universe. Are they going to come back one day and visit us? Take an interest in us? Help us? Not necessarily. Hundreds of thousands of generations have passed for them. Many aren't even aware that we exist.

Imagine when the first British settled in the Americas hundreds of years ago. Fast forward to today and imagine someone asking, "Are they going to come back one day and visit us? Take an interest in us? Help us?" And you get the ridiculousness of the notion. Sure, the odd historian might take an interest and travel to England to find out about his ancestors. But other than that, the colonies have their own business to attend to. The only ones who have a real interest in our development are the ones who originally created us in their own image. That's right, they don't look much different from us. The Bible's creation story says that we were "created in the image of the Elohim". The Hebrew word for God, "Elohim" is nowadays translated as a singular "God" but it's actually a plural word and indicates a group of beings. This, in my view, is a spiritual-extraterrestrial hybrid race of super advanced beings. Hence, the book of Genesis in the Bible says "we created humans in OUR image". However, in spite of us being created by "Gods" rather than "God", it was made sure that the predominant cultural beliefs align with the monotheism of *one* true God. Why? Because the Creators do not want to be worshipped, and because our souls really were all created by one and the same original *Source* of everything else. If you recall the game analogy, focusing on that which ultimately transcends the game is one of the ways to leave the game.

The Serpent race was expelled from the spiritual realm by the Creators and they descended into lower density physical universe and later into the prison-like reality of the lower-astral realms. The entire astral realm was created as a type of holding pattern preventing ascension after death for those unworthy of it. Higher astral realms however, are populated by beings who are on their way upward and may, through proper conduct break through once again to the spiritual plane. To put this into the game context: Some gamers souls had become contaminated from the game, so they had to be put into indefinite quarantine before they could ascend. Those who have difficulty ascending back to the spiritual realm are still playing out the game scenarios in the astral realm.

Here is where it gets really interesting: One of the multifold purposes of Planet Earth is to provide an incarnational point for these lost or trapped souls to incarnate, get another chance to improve so that they can ascend after they die! Imagine consciousness on a scale from 1 to 10, with lower astral beings at level 1. Their incarnation on Earth can allow them to ascend to level 5, where they have a chance to leave the trap. This is why some negativity is welcomed on Planet Earth. Negativity at level 3 and 4 is coming from those who were previously at level 1 and 2 and are struggling to ascend. This is why you will notice a lot of negativity on Earth but almost never *extreme* negativity. When the atomic bombs were detonated over Japan, this was the beginning of a descent into extreme negativity and it was quickly put to a stop so that it wouldn't spread. Curiously, the dropping of those bombs was done in order to stop the equally extreme negativity of Japanese suicide pilots. So a level 1 negativity (genocide through atom bombs) was used to stop level 2 negativity (Japanese suicide bombers). It also stopped World War II. So we are left with a paradox: Without the U.S. atomic bomb, wouldn't World War II just have continued ravishing the world? It's easy to believe so. But those attacks could only be a short-term solution at a great long-term cost. The long-term cost is that nuclear weapons have been hanging over humanitys' heads like a scepter for the last eighty years. I believe World War II could also have been stopped by less negative means. But try explaining this to people who believe that "might is right". In any case, level 1 and 2 negativity are short-lived and taboo on Earth. They contradict this planets pre-programmed purpose.

Approximately 30,000 years ago, according to Australian Aboriginal mythology, the Reptilian beings first arrived on Planet Earth in a manner similar to what the shamanic author above described. From cross-referencing *hundreds* of sources of mostly "new age" literature and reports from past life regression, it seems that, when the Serpent entered, many of our ancestors fled the planet and the entire solar system. The majority of our human ancestors fled to the Pleiadean star system. The humans that stayed behind on Earth, were enslaved by the Serpent empire. As the Serpent ships entered, they directly attacked a Planet that is referred to as "Phaeton" or "Maldek" in alternative science. It was blown to pieces and became what is now known as the Asteroid Belt. On Mars, they only destroyed the cities and surface population and then inhabited the planet for themselves.

Many humans escaped to the Pleiades because they were already familiar with them, having travelled there on several occasions. It was their contingency plan all along. Their stars contain numerous already-created inhabitable planets. Others would be terraformed or cultivated. Once they had regenerated from the war, they built an even more advanced society alongside already present native Pleiadeans. In those days the blue-skinned and the human-skinned did not occupy the same planets but they formed an alliance. Nowadays, there are some mixed planets. The blue-skinned Pleiadeans are native to the star system.

The native Pleiadeans are so peaceful, that the arrival of technologically capable and combat-ready humans came as a blessing to them. These humans were willing to use military force against their common enemies. Their alliance was formed out of necessity. The Blue Beings gave humans some of their higher consciousness, and the humans in return, provided military defense. This is why, in numerous ancient legends, the Pleiades are considered the "protectors of soldiers and warriors". In general, the human-Pleiadeans defense technology is superior to that of the Serpent. The reason they lost our solar system is because they were taken by surprise. Even a superior military can be defeated with the element of surprise. Having learned their lesson, most of the human-populated planets around the Pleiades are now well-equipped and ready for any surprise. The planets themselves have been weaponized.

The alliance lasts to this day. And for this reason, the Pleiadeans (both human and blue) are the most relevant extraterrestrials from our Earth perspective. They know us and they are similar to us but at just a slightly more advanced level. They are our "better selves", the selves we strive to be. I was visited by the blue-skinned Pleiadeans, not by the human Pleiadeans, but I might as well have been visited by either, as both conduct the seeding and population of other planets using Earth DNA.

After Planet Earth was created and seeded with human beings, society once again developed. Approximately 30,000 years ago there was another Reptilian invasion and occupation of Earth. Again, humans fled to the Pleiades and other places. There were only a few left behind — those not involved in space travel. They were farmers and hunters that had no interest in abandoning Earth. These earthbound people were not interested in technology and space-travel, but they were nonetheless attuned to the overall cosmos, so much more than we are today. For instance, this book may seem "fantastical" and "outrageous" to you, but to them it would be about as mundane as a documentary on the Discovery Channel. Most of the world would consider my writings the rants of a madman, out of touch with reality. But I consider most of the world out of touch.

You might say, "Well, there were no advanced humans 30,000 years ago. According to religious scholars, God created humans 6,000 years ago." Or you might say, "Evolution theory and science teaches that the first civilized humans appeared in Sumeria 6,000 years ago." Notice the similarity in the two veils "science" and "religion"? They have both been busy promoting the idea of humankind being around for 6,000 years, against all evidence to the contrary. Fortunately, in recent years, this idea has slowly begun to crumble. But there is still great resistance to the fact that intelligent life didn't just suddenly start 6,000 years ago. Why the falsification of history? Because the Serpent race would like to include Planet Earth in their forced astral quarantine. That only works if we are kept ignorant. Why is the Serpent allowed to keep attacking this planet? It's part of the game-challenge. We are meant to ascend through difficult circumstances.

Around 30,000 years ago, there was another war raging in our solar system and the Serpent had not yet taken full control of Earth. During this time and in thousands of years before that, these simple but peaceful people — our ancestors — built beautiful spiritual societies without the use of technology or even electricity (as we know it) and in perfect harmony with their surroundings. Their ways might be hard to imagine because we think of non-technological people as lacking sophistication, hygiene and civilized life, but it was not that way. They did not need television or the internet because they could see anything they wanted quite clearly by projecting their attention to a place. They did not need phones because they could transfer thoughts. They did not need encryption because they could mask their thoughts from intrusion. They did not need airplanes because they could project their astral body to other locations. Their physical bodies did not travel much for this reason.

In previous books, I called these people *Lemurians.* This is an approximation of what the world looked like back then, pulled from the internet:

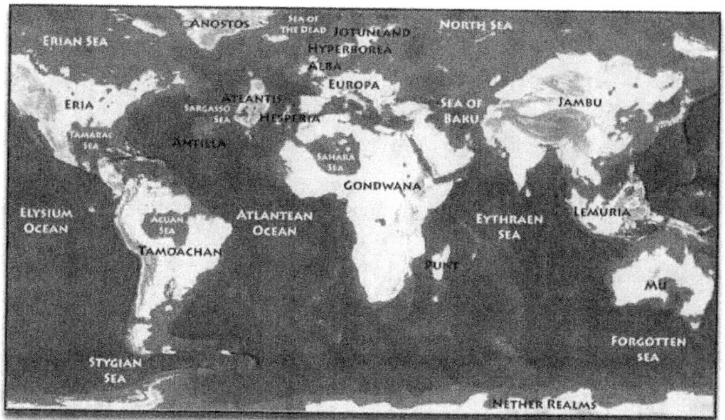

THE CONTINENTS AND MAJOR ISLANDS OF THE ANTIDILUVIAN WORLD

This depiction and many similar, is not entirely accurate. For example, "Mu" and "Lemuria" were the same general places. "Mu" is merely the short form of "Lemuria". But its close enough and the shape of the continents is surprisingly accurate.

While it may not sound flattering, we are the offspring of those left behind. Seen from a higher perspective, our planet is where those souls incarnate that have *karmic issues* to clean up. It's a challenging planet from which a soul learns to ascend either upwards or chooses to further descend. After we die we can either move upwards or go down one of the circles of descent, similar to Dante's Inferno. The reason Earth is interesting to some ETs and NPEs (non-physical-entities) is because it's a planet of choice, a planet of training. The secret purpose of negativity on Earth is to give negative souls an opportunity to ascend. To make this more understandable I'd ask you again to imagine levels of consciousness scale from 1 to 10, with 1 being utterly degenerate, depraved, evil and 10 being completely enlightened. Level 2 is extreme negativity. Level 3 is negative. Therefore, a negative being has the *opportunity*, on Earth, to ascend from his Level 1 state to Level 3. So, if you are asking me "Why can't we just get rid of all negativity on Earth and live in peace?" I ask you: Where should the souls that want to ascend, then go? They'd have nowhere to run, nowhere to learn. Unfortunately, I have yet to read a single book or philosophy talking about this concept. As every human being has a unique insight to offer that nobody else can offer, I think that just may be mine.

There is an *order* to the Universe. Thus, there is also an order to this galaxy. The Galactic Council oversees the various civilizations, races and issues of the "Milky Way". They on the other hand, are overseen by even higher Creator Beings in the spiritual realm. While the spiritual realm is non-dual, the physical allows for duality. Hence, the Serpent is one of the "opposing forces" of this galaxy. It is not the only one, but it is the one hiding out below Earth. The agenda of the literally cold-blooded Reptilians is *survival for the purpose of self-governance outside of the Galactic Council.* They were permitted self-governance, but they used their freedom to subdue and enslave many other civilizations. There are entire stretches of the galaxy that are governed by the nearly emotionless Reptilians and if you were to visit them you'd be horrified at how gloomy and desperate they look. As is typical for lower consciousness, there is no interest in how things aesthetically look and feel, only in functionality. Hence their spaceships have highly advanced functions, but no art, no exotic plants, no music, no fancy design or anything else. When you visit places on Earth that are highly functional but devoid of any love, such as the airport in Riyadh, Saudi Arabia, the city of Ashgabat in Turkmenistan or the buildings of banks and large corporations in the U.S. and you see no sign of love, human creativity, art, music or friendliness you know you are dealing with a negative vibe.

If this whole story sounds familiar to you, that's because the scenarios that play out in our microcosm, also play out in a greater macrocosm. This particular Universe plays out similarly anywhere within it, like a hologram looks similar no matter which angle you view it from. We on Earth behave in a similar manner to many others in the galaxy. In fact, even if this entire book were fiction, you could still learn a lot about everyday life from it, simply by avoiding the mistakes of The Serpent and striving for the attitude of higher beings.

A specific example: the Elohim were upset that they had to destroy the entire planet in a flood for the sake of ridding it from The Serpent. They were upset because they knew that killing innocent life in order to take non-innocent life is wrong. The end does not justify the means. Sacrificing lives "for the greater good" is not for the greater good. If there was a chance that even one single innocent person lived on the Earth that they destroyed, they would have avoided it. So, from that point forward, they vowed to never again destroy the entire planet, but to rise above themselves and find another way to combat The Serpent. How? By recreating humans with the seed and ability to take back their own planet. The classic war of the polarities good and evil is played out throughout the entire Universe. On our Earth and in its greater vicinity, it is played out by The Serpent vs. the Creator-Beings (of which Pleiadeans are a lower-ranking, more physical extension). That's an extremely simplified way of putting the whole story.

When the Reptilians invaded Earth 30,000 years ago, they found non-technological but spiritually-evolved beings and their Kingdom of Lemuria. Its center was in what is now the southwestern Pacific Ocean (Hawaii,

Fiji, Samoa, Tahiti, New Zealand). The Serpent subdued these peaceful people and ruled over them openly and in a despotic manner, destroying Lemuria in the process. They used some humans as slave labor, mostly for mining of gold and other metals. Extensive research on ancient aliens of these times has been done by authors such as Erich von Daniken and Zecharia Sitchin. While Daniken has amassed significantly more hard evidence than Sitchin, Sitchin managed to reconstruct the owner-slave relationship between the "Annunaki" and humans, based on his study of Sumerian Tablets.

Over time and through genetic manipulation, these humans lost their higher consciousness. Eventually, large parts of humanity, worked for them on or off the Earth. Humans who served them unconditionally, rose in their ranks and were able to acquire some level of comfort and fortune for themselves. These humans were placed strategically to govern the regions and projects on behalf of the Serpent. Thus, "royal bloodlines" began. The Empire of Atlantis was built by these more privileged humans that served The Serpent. But as these humans still had some of their former Lemurian spirituality, Atlantis was initially quite beautiful and vastly more advanced than our own "modern" society. It was an almost perfect mix between the higher Lemurian self and the technological Reptilian self. Nonetheless, the Atlantean civilization was tainted from the beginning and their leaders were unhappy because their technological advancements were experienced under oppression from their serpentine overlords.

Because the creativity of humans was partially bound, Atlantis slowly declined over many thousands of years. By the time it was destroyed in the Great Flood approximately 12,000 years ago, most of humanity had degenerated to a point of being unrecognizable as the beautiful beings that the Elohim created. The Serpent agenda on Earth was eventually detected by the Galactic Council and an end was put to their rule with the aforementioned flood.

Humans on Earth in those days, were nothing like their Pleiadean brothers and sisters, which is why they were not considered worth saving. The planet was destroyed, the surviving Reptilians fled into space and the astral realm and only a select few of humans — those who had maintained some of their humanity — were permitted to survive. If you consider this a form of genocide or ethnic cleansing, you misunderstand the lows to which humans had sunk under thousands of years of oppression. Unspeakably vile genetic mutations and cross breeding between animals and humans had taken place. Monstrous creatures were roaming the streets. "Activities" such as cannibalism and unbridled murder were commonplace daily activities and practiced casually in open daylight by the *majority*. The "human" race was on a certain path to *self-extinction.* Why? Because, subconsciously, they'd rather go extinct than continue living under that subtle, yet ever-present serpent oppression. Destroying them with floods and cataclysms served to *shorten their suffering*. Had the flood not taken place, they'd have gone extinct within only a few hundred years on their own.

The Serpent takes a perverse pleasure in humans degrading themselves. The only humans that they supported, were those they could use as slaves or workers in some function. Those that had no usefulness to them, were influenced to degenerate. One of the reasons for this was an *ancient envy*. Humans had been created with a soul, thus having one foot in the spiritual realm, and one in the physical realm. One could say that a human is part angel, part animal. By having humans degrade themselves, the Reptilians could punish the original Creators (or so they thought) and "prove" that the spiritual realm, which they had no access to, is "useless". The whole scenario also served the Creator Beings or Elohim, in that it showed them which humans could strengthen their soul to such a point as to break free from oppression. These humans could then be "harvested" by higher ups for incarnation in better places. You see, if negativity on Earth did not serve a purpose, it wouldn't exist.

As horrifying as their behaviors are to us, to Reptilians they mean nothing, as to them we have no more value than that of worker-ants. They view humanity with contempt and use humans either as tools or squash them. Humans under their psychic influence become psychopaths or serial killers. In fact, one way for a human to "show allegiance" to them, is by committing atrocities that prove they no longer have emotion. As many Reptilians do not have much emotion, a human is considered to "become more like them" by also giving up on any feeling or empathy. It is *empathy* that connects us to the Spiritual Realms and loss of it disconnects us. The original meaning of the religious "Hell" is an alignment with the Serpent and their ghastly arid and humid worlds that are full of suffering and pain. If you align with them during your time on earth, you incarnate into one of their worlds after you pass away. On the other hand, there are also those of the Serpent that begin developing human emotion, after spending too much time with them. Contagion works both ways. Some became traitors to their people and helped humanity in secret. The Serpent living inside Earth are viewed as "soft" compared to those living in other parts of the galaxy or even outside of it, because they have been contaminated by human emotion. It has therefore become a policy to exchange some of their staff on Earth every few hundreds of years.

Permission for the flood and thus the destruction of the Serpent outpost on Earth, was given by the Creators and carried out by the Pleiadeans. The Serpent fled the solar system or were locked into astral limbo and the few remaining humans on Earth, once again lived in peace. After the flood, around one million humans, scattered over Earth, survived. This is reflected in the biblical story of Noah, but also in the stories of many other cultures. The surviving humans were especially selected by the Creators for their resilience to withstand the Serpent programming. It was desired that this unique species of human survive, even though they, too, had greatly degenerated under the Serpent rule. The center of the new Earth, after the flood, spread out from an area around what is today known as Eastern Turkey and Georgia. Humanity reset.

As already described in detail in my books on Atlantis, with the flood also came the destruction of all technology that had been provided by the Serpent. We were set back into an innocent state. This is the only period the cult of Scientism focuses on when they describe how we were stone-age "hunter-gatherers". In order to maintain this version of our ancient "history", all artifacts that prove otherwise, are collected and hidden. If you don't believe that, research how quickly "the government" appears on the scene when archaeologists dig up something new. And if it is not collected and hidden, then it is dismissed by the "new Inquisition" of Scientism. And if it is even too late to hide or dismiss it, then slight "corrections" are made in the supposed timeline of our history, but often without receiving any publicity.

A few decades ago, it was taught with certainty in our "universities" that that there were no high civilizations more than 6,000 years ago. This date has consecutively been "corrected" because of "new discoveries" (discoveries they were too late to cover up). The date soon became 8,000 years ago. Then 10,000 years ago. Then 30,000 years ago. Now they are finally admitting that there were civilized people 60,000 years ago. Then they have the audacity to pretend that they never made previous claims with absolute certainty. The behavior of these "institutions of higher learning" shows patterns of pathological liars, in which they keep correcting their versions of the story as new evidence emerges. Any parent who has ever witnessed a lying child, knows these patterns. Had they said "As far as we know, there was no civilization 6,000 years ago" rather than making the idea mandatory across all curriculums and schools, it would have been a different story. There would have been room for exploration. Suppression of knowledge occurs when no room for exploration is given, due to dogma. Even as a child, I questioned many of the things our teachers taught us. Often, one could tell, that questioning was not welcome, because they themselves had been indoctrinated into fixed ways of seeing things. My history teacher kept repeating the lie that "Columbus discovered America". The curious and informed kid I was, I said, "What about the Vikings? There is evidence that the Vikings were here before." But I was told that if I write that as an answer on the test, I would get points deducted. Not to mention the natives that were already there. Wasn't it *they* who discovered America? And didn't the Maya also venture into North America? I like to cite "Columbus discovered America" as an example, but there are thousands of others I could cite. Such as the preposterous idea that the ancients were not seafaring and could not cross the oceans. Or that all tales of beings flying in the sky were fiction because flight was not possible. History as taught in school was and still widely is a scam. Books such as these and many others, are an attempt to work around the scam and try to piece together what we know. And while the cult of Scientism may scoff at books like these, I scoff at their long-held assertion that "Columbus discovered America" and a few thousand other falsehoods.

Even though the majority of humanity were thrown back into the "stone age" state after the flood, there were a few who remembered and preserved the technology, in secret. Remnants of pre-flood time were stowed away in caverns or stashed in remote forests or taken away for hiding. That was the dawn of secret societies, their purpose being, to preserve the Serpent knowledge and use it to their advantage and to rule over the uninformed crowds. Some of them sought to continue their reign through the remains of the previous Serpent kingdom and the few crumbs of knowledge that survived the flood. Anyone exploring subterranean caves more deeply, would find forgotten remains from pre-flood times. Some of the devices would even still be functional. Yes, some technology is of such high quality that it lasts for tens of thousands of years. Much unlike our laptops that are designed to break down after only a few years.

In fact, there have been tales of explorers who accidentally stumbled upon strange and inexplicable things in caves and elsewhere. Oddly shaped lightbulbs that require no electricity found deep within the caves of

New Guinea, for instance. Or strange metal boxes with unknown inscriptions, picked up in 60,000-year-old mining caves in Africa. Such findings are rapidly hushed up. By whom? By the keepers of the pre-flood secret. These secret societies are not known by anyone. All these books we have on "secret" societies contain nothing of value. They are published as a veil. There are several layers of onion that need to be peeled before getting even the slightest glimpse of *actual* secret societies, some of which reside in such remote places on Earth that none of them are ever seen by commoners. Consider for a moment, the planet you are living on. Geologists estimate that there are millions of uninhabited islands, for example. Just like there are millions of square miles of uninhabited lands. Not to mention subterranean lands. It's not that difficult to hide things.

After the flood, as is typical for the benevolent Galactic Council, a "noninterference" law was once again issued for Earth, so that humans could develop on their own. The Serpent empire does not believe in non-imposition, they believe in *conditioning* and that humans had to be "trained" and "re-trained" or "programmed" for various tasks.

Reptile vs. Creator attitudes can be found in all of our society, even down to the way you raise your children. The "hands off" approach that allows for kids to develop mostly on their own accord, with a few interventions here and there, is the higher consciousness approach. The total-control and indoctrination approach, is the Reptilian one. This, by the way, is one of the reasons I prefer to use the words "workshop" or "seminar" to the word "training". Training and conditioning are what you do with animals. The only place it is appropriate is when it comes to physical conditioning, sports or skills that require repetition. Skills that require repetition, by the way, are skills of the mind. The soul, with its vast storehouse of knowledge, learns things easily.

Having a non-interference policy in place, both the Creators and their physical Pleiadean representatives once again left Earth and left the solar system, only to check back up on us every few hundreds of years.

Between 12,000 and 5,000 B.C. we resided again in a mostly primitive state.

At around 5,000 B.C., a fleet of the Serpent again returned to Earth. History repeats itself if old lessons are not learned. Seeing that there were neither Pleiadeans nor Creator Beings present, they predictably violated the non-interference treaty once more and also once again started imposing their technology on us. But having been detected and destroyed last time, this time they did so more covertly. It is also no coincidence that they returned. They were called by the very humans that were secretly hoarding the ancient knowledge of these beings. We are not victim to any outside force. We experience what we call upon ourselves. Even those humans that did not call upon the Serpent, were nonetheless complicit in the covert takeover of their planet through their own passive attitude. The innocent people on Earth, did not care enough about developing awareness and learning about the larger nature of the Universe. They were therefore subject to manipulation from outside. The bearers of the ancient technological secrets saw how undeveloped and passive the normal populace was, so they assumed that the creators of those technologies were superior. And so they aligned themselves with them. It just felt much more exciting to welcome fiery flying spaceships and their dragon pilots than to pick cotton in the fields. And that type of thinking is one of the classical errors of humanity — to think that just because someone has technology or money that they are "superior". They might be superior in technology, but they are not necessarily superior ethically or spiritually.

The new strategy through which the Serpent could avoid extinction, was by taking humans hostage. They were aware of the Creator Beings decree to never destroy Earth again. If they could occupy the interior of Earth and have a few of their worshippers lead humans while not degenerating them to the point they had before (but just enough to enslave and use them), they could reign while using humans as shields against Pleiadean attack. The Creators loved humanity and required Earth for the purpose of karmic ascension. Within a greater game context, if the Creators could help humanity achieve prosperity and enlightenment, then the Creators themselves could be awarded the next level of their own evolution. This is why they had *promised* not to destroy humanity again by giving them the tools and knowledge they needed to become civilized and survive.

Staying undetected (or so they thought), the Serpent receded from public view. They did not fly their fiery aircraft around. They did not support sudden technological jumps in humanity. They merely occupied the inside of Earth, sold off human DNA to other extraterrestrial races and operated mostly from the astral realm through remote influence of their leaders and the use of strange psychotronic devices. They let power hungry and attention-needy humans rule the planet for them. Their endgame is still to degenerate humankind, but in a manner undetected by the Creators, so that they will only realize it when it's too late. The amusing thing about all of this is that both the Creator Beings (who made this planet and our bodies) were fully aware from the beginning of the Reptilian presence on Earth. They *allowed* them to be here. It was part of *their* plan. They will allow them to be here, until humanity finds the strength to transcend them. This is no different than having a bunch of unpleasant bugs in your house. They will be there until you clean up. And if you clean up without extinguishing what attracts them, they will return after you clean up. As long as humans choose negative thoughts and deeds, they will attract negative occupation. It's really a training school: Put the adversary on Earth, so that humans grow to transcend the adversary. No adversary, no growth. From this you can see that evil serves its purpose. Evil is not just there for the sake of evil, but as a tool to learn to handle it, deal with it and finally overcome it. You can then easily become a member of very high spiritual realms because you have learned to neutralize negative influence.

The kings, pharaohs and leaders were not the Serpent (as generally claimed in conspiracy literature) themselves, but some of them were indoctrinated in the Serpent ways and often controlled on an astral level. The Serpent is not allowed to rule *as* human, only over them. And only if those humans consent to it. This is their limitation, so the whole ridiculous game has been to trick humans into consent to being oppressed. Some of them were able to withstand the Serpent indoctrination and do much good for humanity. Some of them carry traces of Reptilian blood due to sexual relations between humans and these creatures. Some of the ruling elite are part of the Serpent system (not all, as conspiracy theorists claim), some are actually of Pleiadean lineage and then there are those rulers who are genuinely human and uninfluenced by either side. If you see a ruler engage in wholesale mass slaughter, such as Genghis Khan, you'll know he is psychically influenced by the Serpent. For thousands of years, various power players on Earth have been competing for dominance, within rules imposed by the Creator Beings. Nobody can alter rules set by a higher level of consciousness. The only ways those rules can be subverted is by ascending to those levels just long enough to change the rules. As you can imagine, this too has been attempted. The cosmic play of agents, double-agents, darkness posing as light and light posing as darkness goes on just like it happens among our smaller scale secret agencies. Spiritual enlightenment is a state of transcending many levels and leaving all those games behind. Losing interest in all these games and conflicts is one of the first steps upward.

In pre-flood times some of the human kings were said to be “descendants of the gods”. These were actually Reptilian-human hybrids. Society under them was structured in strict dictatorial hierarchy, similar to the caste system. The Galactic Council and our Pleiadean allies, on the other hand, are more similar to the U.S. system of a republic. Our planet experiences a balance of Pleiadean influence and Reptilian influence. As hard as it is for many to admit, this is actually wanted by the Galactic Council, as our planet is meant to be a perfect mix of light and darkness. We have 50% negativity by our own volition. Once we are ourselves are aware of and fed up with the Serpent occupation of our planet, we will be rid of them. It’s really as ridiculously simple as that, though many “in the know” will deny it. Through various channellers and drug-induced visions, the Serpent claim that this planet belongs to them. That is only true for as long as we put up with negativity. If there is no enemy within you, no enemy outside of you can harm you.

The Serpent control the lower astral belt around Earth. Their influence is mostly psychic. Physically, they have built cities and spaceship bases below Earth. Pleiadeans have suggested blowing the planet up, just to root out the Reptilians, but the Creator Beings do not want us destroyed. Therefore, there is a sort of silent agreement between the Serpents and Creator Beings that the Reptilians do not mess with our free will. In return, the Galactic Council and Pleiadeans will not seek to destroy them. If the Reptilians have influence over humans, it is only through the *consent* of the human. Conspiracy books on the Reptilians claim, that they can enslave us without our consent, but this is not true. If it were, we'd be living in a much, much worse world already. Therefore, their game is to weaken humans to a point, where they give up their free will or consent to being used by them. Thus, they keep in line with their deal with the Galactic Council, but at the same time maintain control of this planet.

Depictions of the Reptilian "gods" can be seen all over the planet, especially in the ancient Mayan, Asian and Hindu cultures that depict dragons on their temples, statues and paintings. These depictions recall a time when the Reptilians were still more physical. Over the last few thousand years, they have slowly and gradually provided us with knowledge in mathematics, astrology, medicine and engineering so that we may build more civilized societies. They thus present themselves as great teachers and helpers of society, bringers of enlightenment if only we were to give up our connection to the spiritual realm and join them in theirs.

The Creator Beings and Pleiadeans, on the other hand, have not provided technology but rather spiritual guidance in the form of sages, saints and prophets sent to Earth. Why? Because they know that technology without higher consciousness is self-destructive. If you give the child-like Earthlings only technology without empathy, they will eventually destroy themselves. The Serpent have a keen understanding of human nature and know this. It is their hope that we destroy ourselves "out of our own free will". They want it to look like we are to blame for our self-destruction, which is why they have introduced technological progress ever so slowly. Why do they want us to destroy ourselves? Because they are not allowed to destroy us. We are like pesky bugs to them, that they have to put up with. It is their hope that if we destroy ourselves, the Creator Beings will feel remorse and sadness and change their attitude toward the Reptilians (apart from the prospect of taking over Planet Earth, the interior of which provides ideal living conditions for them). Another long-term plan of theirs is to use humans under their control, to infiltrate Pleiadean society. But that's a story for another time lest this book get too bizarre.

That is not to say that without them we would never have developed civilized society or technology. We would have, and there are plenty of inventions that are human-made. Inventions however that have great destructive potential, especially weapons, are influenced by the Serpent. They feel great glee at the destructive force of these weapons. On the other hand, there are Serpent-factions which oppose total obliteration of the human race because they could then no longer use them as playthings and labor-slaves. And then there are the contaminated Reptilians who actually side with and support humans. But these are a minority.

How did the Reptilians come to occupy the interior of the Earth? Originally some of them escaped the flood in deep caverns. Today, the climate conditions of inner Earth are good for them. They cannot survive for a very long time on Earth's surface because it's too cold and dry. Their ideal climate is hot and humid, in fact no different than that of a common snake.

Later, others settled there in order to avoid detection through the Pleiadeans. The Pleiadeans know that Earth is again occupied by them, so their stay there is simply to use human shields to protect against any Pleiadean attack and also because these have been their established bases for thousands of years. In an interstellar context, Pleiadeans have already gained the upper hand against them for several hundred years. There are very few places where they can safely stay in physical form.

Another reason they keep their presence hidden is because humans are easier to manipulate as long as they *don't know* who they are manipulated by. Throughout history, we have projected many as "the enemy" but seen from a higher vantage point, there is only one enemy: The Reptilian presence on Earth. Jews, Muslims, Christians, Germans, Americans, Iranians, Japanese, Chinese, Russians, etc. are not "the enemy". The Reptilian manipulation of the human psyche tempts humans to see each other as "the enemy" in order to conceal the true nemesis. However, and I repeat this, in order not to fall into the same trappings of the contemporary conspiracy-theorist: Ultimately it is our choice to be manipulated, our choice to wage war, our choice to suffer, even if the Reptilians gleefully enjoy guiding us in those directions.

In the last thirty years, the consciousness of humanity made a jump upwards, *through our own efforts.* This means that humans are no longer as easy to manipulate at the astral or psychic level. They no longer as easily fall into fear and confusion. Entity possession, a phenomenon where a non-physical being completely takes over a human body, is becoming increasingly rare and improbable.

Some readers may be stunned or shocked at how "far out" and "crazy" this author sounds by now, especially considering that his previous books all sounded fairly rational. But rest assured, for me, these topics are no big deal. I have been aware of the Serpent since childhood. I have been aware of positive aliens since childhood (even though I only recently learned that the blue-skinned ones are Pleiadean). And even though reading this book probably makes either for great entertainment or for "the most shocking revelations imaginable", rest assured that the Reptilians, Pleiadeans and other aliens do not figure that high on my priority list. To me, this whole saga is happening on the periphery of my own life. My soul came to this planet to experience this planet and I have many beautiful projects throughout a day to keep me happily occupied. I do not dwell on these subjects, am not mystified or entranced by them, and obviously do not talk about them much (this is my 25th book and only now do I mention the Earth's overall situation. As I write this, it occurs to me that 2+5 = 7, so I guess it just had to be the 25th). What is truly important is raising your consciousness. But telling you the full story will support you in understanding just how important that is. By elevating your own level of consciousness, you are, frankly, saving humanity.

Most surface dwellers are completely oblivious to the fact that there is an entire society being run inside Earth. They'd be surprised to find entire subway systems, infrastructures and spaceports outside of their view. Major cities even have elevators that go deep underground. This has all been extensively documented and backed up through official government papers by researchers like Richard Sauder and many others, and yet most still have never heard of such a thing. That's because those who don't believe in such possibilities, filter out any evidence of them.

When I asked the Pleiadeans who appeared to me at night who they were purchasing my DNA from, I can only surmise that it was from the temporary rulers of this world. Upon further research for this book, it became clear to me that they actually sell human genetic material to various alien races. People who are strong and healthy or have extrasensory abilities are the most sought after for blood. Even Pleiadeans apparently purchase from them — their enemy — in order to populate new worlds with our DNA. They have no choice but to pay the Serpent, since, by treaty, they are the rulers of Earth. And again, as unflattering as it sounds, we are apparently viewed by both our friends and enemies as cattle for harvest. The Galactic Council allows these trades to happen because human DNA is considered good. The Pleiadeans terraform hundreds of new worlds every decade. Many of these new worlds are from spaces conquered from the Serpent empire. Most Serpents are eliminated by the Pleiadeans, but some are kept alive and employed by them. The scenario is really not that much different than on Earth. For example, in World War II, the Germans and Americans were considered enemies. Individuals from both countries nonetheless did business with each other. And after the war, Americans employed many former German scientists rather than killing or imprisoning them.

Smart beings would rather use us than kill us, unless absolutely necessary for self-defense. If the "enemy" can be reasoned with in any way, he needn't be killed. The problem with most of the Serpent is that any sort of leniency is quickly punished. But there are a few who are reasonable enough to choose life over death. From what I can tell, the Blue-Skinned Beings do not kill at all. Prior to the arrival of humans within their star system, they camouflaged their presence and cities any time the Serpent fleets would pass by. Sometimes they'd be detected and attacked. Many attacks were unsuccessful, due to the higher energy the Blue Beings radiated. Nonetheless the attacks were emotionally painful, so they learned to evade and avoid the Serpent. A peaceful people would rather become invisible to the enemy than counter-attack. Out of sight, out of mind. But since that enemy didn't give up, the arrival of spacefaring humans was welcomed.

Even though Pleiadeans are generally benevolent, due to our ignorance, many do not view us positively. Their benevolence prevents them from imposing on humans and harvesting human materials directly, but they do purchase it from the Serpent in exchange for some immunity from annihilation. If it weren't for the Pleiadeans, the Serpent would have destroyed humanity long ago. Some of our world leaders are under remote psychotronic and astral influence from them (which is the main reason Pleiadeans do not establish diplomatic relationships with our "leaders"). There are, however, a few covert Pleiadean influences on Earth. These are through spiritual communication with certain individuals who are able to receive their transmissions.

Most books on these subjects emphasize the Serpent side of things, which is why this one will emphasize our Pleiadean friends. Yet another "ancient aliens" book on the wise serpents of Sumeria is not needed, just like another conspiracy book is not needed. Not to mention that "conspiracy" is the wrong word. Our killing and eating of animals is no conspiracy — it's just what we, as a species do. The negativism of the Reptilian race is not a conspiracy, it's just who they are. So without further ado, let's shift attention our more interesting beings.

CHAPTER SIX

THE PLEIADES CONNECTION TO EARTH

Books on the Pleiades are rare. *Coherent* books rarer still. But signs of their presence can be found throughout the world in every culture, both ancient and modern. This chapter presents these signs to the best of my knowledge. I have collected references to the Pleiades from religion, mythology, New Age spirituality and popular culture. I will keep speculation minimal, focusing mostly on hard facts. You can make up your own mind about what they mean. While writing this book, I read several books on the subject, hoping to glean additional data from them, but I found almost *nothing* in those books because authors tend to get lost in several layers of speculation.

An example: Let's say a remote Amazonian tribe depicted the seven stars in one of their cave paintings. They claim that their ancestors depicted those stars because that's where their "gods" came from. Okay, fine. So we try to date when the picture was made, to find out whether it really is ancient. Then we try to corroborate the story by digging through legends of this tribe and those nearby. Satisfied with the results, one might then speculate that this is evidence of a prehistoric visitation by Pleiadeans. If I were to add another layer of speculation to this, I might say that this particular tribe is descended from Pleiadeans. Once accepting that line of thought, I might claim that their practice of painting their houses blue is a sign of their royal Pleiadean ancestry. I might then find that one of their symbols is a spiral and claim that this represents a wormhole by which they will return to their home in the stars. I might then say that the number of dots etched into the spiral represent a calendar with which we can predict the exact date of their return through the interstellar wormhole.

You see the problem in getting caught up in too much speculation? It never ends and you lose track of what is actually true, so that in the end anything could be true. When anything could be true, it eventually doesn't matter what is true and interest is lost. Agents of false information can easily muddy the waters of clear thinking by overwhelming attention and credibility in this way.

On the other hand, too little speculation is also a problem, because you never allow yourself to put two and two together, even if its staring in your face. In the example above, I might say, "Well, they just saw the Pleiades in the sky and drew it on their cave paintings. And then they made up a story about those stars. Nothing to see here."

The journey of truth-finding requires a balance between too strict of a reductionism and too vast of a conjecture.

The Pleiades in Abrahamic Religion

Unbeknownst to many, the Pleiades along with their accompanying Orion constellation, are the *only* star-systems mentioned in the Bible *several* times. Why would a book, of which we say it is said to have been "written by God" specifically single out the Pleiades? Amongst the thousands of stars that are visible with the eye, why these?

Amos 5:8: in the Old Testament, says:

Seek him that makes the seven stars and Orion, and turns the shadow of death into the morning, and makes the day dark with night: that calls for the waters of the sea, and pours them out upon the face of the earth: The Lord is his name.

Job 9:9 in the Old Testament says:

He is the Maker of the Bear and Orion, the Pleiades and the constellations of the south.

God being the maker of all stars, why single out that he is the maker of the Pleiades? Unless of course, there is some kind of coded message in that.

Job 38:31 of the New Testament says:

Can you bind the sweet influences of Pleiades, or loose the bands of Orion?

The last quote is from the King James Bible written centuries ago. Newer translations have replaced "sweet influences of the Pleiades" with "chains of the Pleiades", which quite openly changes their meaning.

The "New International Version" of the Bible, for example, says:

"Can you bind the chains of the Pleiades? Can you loosen Orion's belt?

Using internet Bible-comparison tools, I have found that this kind of change from older Bible versions is actually common. Looking more deeply, I have also found that most of these "updated" translations are unwarranted. If we consider that the rulers of this planet are anti-Pleiadean, maybe it's no coincidence that positive Pleiadean influence would be reversed into something negative.

Revelation 1:20 of the New Testament has this to say:

The mystery of the seven stars which you saw in my right hand, and the seven golden candlesticks. The seven stars are the angels of the seven churches: and the seven candlesticks which you saw are the seven churches.

The Bible, in other words, acknowledges that the Pleiades (the 7 Stars), are angels — which is a way of saying they are *forces of good.* Somehow, I doubt your regular priest or pastor has mentioned the Pleiades or explained why they would be the "seven churches". Religions are full of esotericism that is never learned in the exoteric (public).

The original Hebrew word that was translated as Pleiades is *Kimah.* It is referred to in the Talmud and Midrash as the 7-star-system. Rabbinic scholars generally agree that Kimah is the Pleiades, even though there are some that would like Kimah to refer to the Draco constellation (which is historically linked to the dragon, or, which is in other words, the Serpent).

One of the obvious reasons the Pleiades have played a significant role with our ancestors is because they can be seen with the naked eye from Earth. Well, *six* of them can be seen clearly and the seventh only with strain. I have the notion that once we live in an enlightened world, we will be able to see the seventh star more clearly. The star-system is approximately 400 lightyears far away, which is not really that much when compared to the size of the Universe or even just the galaxy. Actually, the Pleiades are not only seven stars but a constellation of *hundreds*. They are referred to as the seven stars because that is how we see them from Earth. In fact, the Talmud, thousands of years ago, already confirmed that the Pleiades had "about 100 important stars", long before we could see so in our modern telescopes. Where could the Jews possibly have gotten such knowledge? Well, they say they got it from Moses. And Moses says he got it from God. I believe such accurate data was given to Moses to underline the legitimacy of their source. "Let's give humans some data they will find out in thousands of years, then they'll know we were the real thing."

In Rabbinic literature, the Kimah are curiously linked to the Flood, which ties in to my claim that the Flood was initiated by the Pleiadeans. According to Professor Stern (1864) of Goettingen:

'Rabbi Joshua [in the Talmud, Rosh Hashshanah, p. 11], in speaking of the Flood, says that the rain began on the seventeenth day of the month Iyar, on which Kimar is accustomed to rise in the morning, and the springs begin to dry up. In consequence of the perverse 238ehavior of men, God also changed the order of the universe: in place of its morning rising, He caused Kimah to set in the morning, and removed two stars from it: the springs swelled and the Flood took place. According to Rabbi Eliezer, these changes took place on the seventeenth day of the month

Marheshvan, when Kimah is accustomed to set in the morning, and the springs increase. God reversed the order of the universe: Kimah rose on the morning of that day, and lost two stars. The springs continued to increase and the Flood took place.'

Moreover, the Midrash that say that "God brought on the deluge, by displacing two stars in the constellation of Kimah *(Midrash ha-Gadol, p. 156).*

Could this be a reference to two Starfleet's being deployed from the Pleiades to cause floods on Earth? This may sound far-fetched to you, but that's how it was communicated to me during my own Pleiadean experience.

In Islamic culture, the Pleiades are known as al-Thurayya. The ancient Arabs used the Pleiades to predict the weather, as navigation and to determine seasons for agriculture.

Prophet Mohammed is said to have mentioned the Pleiades. A Hadith by Iman Bukhari says:

*A companion of The Holy Prophet (may the peace and blessings of Allah be upon him) relates: One day we were sitting with The Holy Prophet (may the peace and blessings of Allah be upon him) when this chapter was revealed. I enquired from Muhammad (may the peace and blessings of Allah be upon him). Who are the people to whom the words "and among others of them who have not yet joined them"** refer? Salman (may Allah be pleased with him), a Persian was sitting among us. The Holy Prophet (may the peace and blessings of Allah be upon him) put his hand on Salman (may Allah be pleased with him) and said. If faith were to go up to the Pleiades, a man from among these would surely find it. (Bukhari).*

It is not entirely clear what this verse actually means. Common interpretations say that it refers to Salman's people being so wise that if anything were happening in the Pleiades, then they would know of it. He is using the

Pleiades to praise the Persians. He is essentially saying that knowledge of the Pleiades is among our most precious and secret.

The three major Abrahamic religions all refer to the Pleiades in a positive tone, associating them with God, with divine secret knowledge, with angels and with churches.

I did not know of their good reputation before starting this book. In fact, I had difficulty finding *any* negative reference to the Pleiades at all. Apparently the Pleiadeans have a good PR department.

The Pleiades in Mythology and Ancient Culture

The word "Pleiades" itself derives from Greek mythology, where the star cluster was associated with the "Seven Sisters" (wives of "the Gods) which are:

- Maia, wife of Zeus, meaning mother, nurse or "the great one"
- Electra, wife of Zeus, meaning bright, amber or shining.

- Taygete, wife of Zeus, meaning long-necked.
- Alcyone, wife of Poseidon, meaning "The Queen who wards off evil"
- Celaeno, wife of Poseidon and Promotheus, meaning dark-skinned or tanned.
- Sterope (or Asterope) wife of Areas, meaning twinkling, lightning.
- Merope wife or Sisyphus, meaning eloquent or bee-eater.

The Wikipedia entry has this to say:

After Atlas was forced to carry the heavens on his shoulders, Orion began to pursue all of the Pleiades, and Zeus transformed them first into doves, and then into stars to comfort their father. The constellation of Orion is said to still pursue them across the night sky.

My view of Greek mythology is that it is coded language to describe ancient history with astonishing accuracy as well as alignment with what we know from other ancient "myths" and religions. "Doves" are frequently used as a symbol for souls or spirits, indicating that The Blue-Skinned Pleiadean Beings were first purely spiritual before they descended into the physical Universe and "became stars". Seen from the perspective of Levels of Energy or consciousness, everything either ascends upwards into increasing levels of non-physicality or downwards into increasing density. The Pleiades are a level "less dense" than ours and a level more dense than the Spiritual Realm.

According to Greek mythology, originally all seven stars could be seen clearly, but Electra, the seventh star, *veiled herself from view to mortals* after the burning of Troy. She is considered "the lost Pleiad".

The Pleiades likely comes from the Greek Peleiades, meaning *flock of doves.* It is possible that for this reason, doves have come to symbolize peace in Judaism, Christianity and some pagan beliefs. In Christianity, the dove symbolizes "The Holy Spirit", which transformed into a dove when it descended upon Jesus Christ.

What is the "Holy Spirit"? It is the biblical word for what we would call "The Field" or "Consciousness" or "Cosmic Energy" or "Life Force". When it descends to one frequency lower, it crystallizes into a discernable object, star or point of light, in this case symbolized by doves.

If I am correct that the Pleiades play an important role in our history, then they should be expected to be represented in *every* culture on Earth. And sure enough, they are.

Norse mythology says that the Pleiades were the hens of the goddess Freyja. This again, distantly echoes the Pleiades alliance with the good and with the highest authorities of the galaxy. Freyja, meaning "the lady" is associated with beauty, fertility, gold and war. She took half of all warriors who died honorably, whereas the other half went to Odin's Valhalla (which, in my view, is an even higher realm, equivalent to Heaven or "The Field"). After Sweden was Christianized, statues and reverence of Freya was replaced with Virgin Mary, the "Queen of Heaven", due to their equivalency.

Baltic mythology personifies the Pleiades as a benevolent brother who helps orphan girls marry and assists soldiers walking on fields. The theme of assisting soldiers and warriors is recurring throughout the world. I ascribe this to the fact that our Pleiadean ancestors were actually warriors and have been waging a galactic war against the Serpent for a long time.

In Ukrainian folklore the word for Pleiades also means "hundredfold glowing" or" a hundred embers" echoing the ancient Jewish knowledge of a hundred important starts. According to Ukrainian legend, once long ago there lived seven maids. They liked to dance and sing in honor of the gods. After their death, they were turned into the seven stars.

In Hungarian, the name for the constellation is "a hen with chicks", mirroring other cultures association of the Pleiades with hens and birds. If you have read my books on Atlantis, you won't be surprised at ancient accounts across the globe all telling similar stories. Rather than being "coincidental", this means that they all originate from the same true sources and were passed down from generation to generation. *Scientism* has done humanity a great disservice in acting as if none of these accounts have anything to do with reality.

The indigenous peoples of the Americas have a lot to say about the seven stars. For them it was common to test keenness of vision by the number of stars one could see in the constellation. The Andean culture of South America, linked the Pleiades to *abundance*, because they return to the Southern Hemisphere sky each year at harvest time. The Aztecs of Mexico based their calendar upon the Pleiades. The Native Americans of the Cherokee, The Lakota, the Barfoot tribe, the Mono, and the Cheyenne have dozens of legends and stories around the Pleiades.

The Hopi tribe not only had stories about the Pleiades, but also about beings from there, flying in "Kachina" spacecraft. Hopi rituals are scheduled by observing the Pleiades.

An ancient prophecy of the Hopi Natives of America states: *"When the Blue Star Kachina makes its appearance in the Heavens, the Fifth World will emerge."* According to Hopi legend, the Kachina are flying aircraft. The aircraft that will bring about the New World, or the next higher level of consciousness, is from the "Blue Star", which according to them, is the star Sirius. It struck me that the Hopi know this. It confirms my own information and research that the Blue Pleiadean Beings, originated on Sirius before they migrated and descended (the right word would be "descend-migrated") to the Pleiades. The Pleiadean Star System is one energy-level down from that of Sirius. Sirius plays a significant role in some elite circles on Earth that are familiar with the nature of reality and our way back home. In fact, it is my view that the term "blue blooded", as used by those who consider themselves "royals" is not due to their veins being blue, but due to their desired connection to these beings. You'd be surprised to learn how obsessed some of these "royals" are with descendances and bloodlines. As explained earlier in the book, the genetic makeup of the physical body or the bloodline is not nearly as important as the spiritual attitude of a person. In fact, certain royalty secretly believe that they are descendant from various extraterrestrials and divinely chosen to be above the rest of humanity. To keep their blood "pure", much inbreeding has occurred. As we know today, through genetic sciences, inbreeding causes mental and physical degeneracy rather than elevation. It's all about level of consciousness, not bloodline.

The ancient cultures of Guatemala, such as the Monte Alto, Ujuxte and Takalik Abaj, built their observatories using the Pleiades as reference. They called them the seven sisters and believed them to be *the land they originated from.* Interestingly, the Monte Alto culture, which predates the mysterious Olmec culture, also built gigantic head statues such as the Olmec did, has the oldest known magnetic artifacts in the world.

From the Wikipedia Page:

Many of the Monte Alto sculptures are magnetic as well. Since certain distinctive patterns of magnetism recur with some frequency, it would appear that the sculptures were executed by artisans who were aware of these properties. If this is true, the Monte Alto sculptures no doubt deserve recognition as the oldest known magnetic artifacts in the world.

Of the collection of "potbellies" sculptures from Monte Alto on display in the town park of La Democracia, Guatemala and in front of its local museum, Museo Regional de Arqueología de la Democracia, four of the heads and three of the bodies were found to have magnetic properties. All four of the heads have a north magnetic pole located in their right temples, while three of them have south magnetic poles below the right ear and the fourth (that in front of the museum) has a south magnetic pole in its left temple. Such a pattern of occurrence is unlikely to be a matter of chance, even in a sample size as small as four.

Source:

https://en.wikipedia.org/wiki/Monte_Alto_culture

A tour through the Museum of Paleontology of Monte Alto, features an array of alien-looking structures, including Reptilian ones which are labelled as "dinosaurs" (if you recall my books on Atlantis, you may remember that I believe that "dinosaurs" is a modern invention to mask the existence of the Serpent race).

Of course, the cult of Scientism and their contrived "history" will tell you that Dinosaurs and Humans did not co-exist and that these Reptilians were far, far older than any human cultures. Many "dinosaur" remains were dug up in the Monte Alto region. Some archaeologists have said that these remains were dug up alongside artifacts of the Pleiadean-aligned Monte Alto culture, indicating that there may have been some co-existence as well as an awareness of the intergalactic war between the Pleiades and the Serpent.

These are some of the artifacts of the Monte Alto culture. I display them here because they have a distinctly unearthly feel to them:

The Nez Perce, native people of Idaho, have a myth that mirrors that of many other cultures, including the Greek. It is amazing enough that an ancients of America have so many significant stories in common with the Greeks (as you'll recall from my books on Atlantis). They are essentially the same stories with the difference that the Greek once were more meticulously preserved because they were put into writing rather than only being passed on through oral transmission.

According to Wikipedia:

In the Nez Perce version the Pleiades is also a group of sisters, however the story itself is somewhat different. One sister falls in love with a man and, following his death, is so absorbed by her own grief that she tells her sisters about him. They mock her and tell her how silly it is of her to feel sad for the human after his death, and she in return keeps her growing sadness to herself, eventually becoming so ashamed and miserable about her own feelings that she pulls the sky over her face like a veil, blocking herself from view. This myth explains why there are only six of the seven stars visible to the naked eye.

The Pleiades play a central role in Navajo folklore and ritual as well as their Creation Story.

From Wikipedia (bolding mine):

According to one version of the Navajo creation story, Black God is first encountered by First Man and First Woman on the Yellow (third) world. Black God is, first and foremost, a fire god. He is the inventor of the fire drill and was the first being to discover the means by which to generate fire…

The creation story of the Navajo people is recounted as part of a Blessingway Ritual: "The Sky and the Earth were placed after the People emerged from a series of previous worlds. Four Holy People – First Man, First Woman, Salt Woman, and Black God – [sat together and] ***planned the conditions of life on the surface of the earth.*** *" Still more, these four figures are collectively responsible, not just for the organization of all things terrestrial, but for the placement of the stars themselves. Of the four, however, because of his association with fire, the Navajo saw Black God as responsible for the creation, and sustaining of the celestial bodies. As the story goes, First Man, First Woman, Salt Woman were sitting in a hogan (a Navajo hut made of wood and dirt)* ***when Black God entered with the constellation of Pleiades*** *affixed to his ankle. "When several of the Holy People commented on the presence of this constellation, Black God stamped his foot vigorously, bringing the constellation to his knee. A second stamp… brought the stars to his hip." The Holy People were impressed by Black God's display and nodded approvingly. Black God then stamped his foot a third and fourth time, until the constellation was lodged in his temple. Satisfied, Black God declared: "There it shall stay!" The Holy People were so captivated by Black God's performance that they gave him the responsibility* *of creating constellations with which to adorn the "upper dark." Black God acquiesced, carefully arranging his star crystals throughout the heavens until the night sky was beautified by his glittering constellations. Yet, the crystals had no light of their own, and the night sky remained dark. "To solve this problem, Black God placed some of his fire in the sky by providing an igniter star to radiate light for each constellation." Black God went on to impart his fire unto the sun.*

The Constellation of Pleiades** and its placement on the mask of Black God is emblematic of the Navajo philosophy of 'Sa'a naghai bk'e hozho' which **pertains to the Nightway ritual and its fundamental goal of the restoration of balance, beauty, health, and wholeness.

***The constellation Pleiades was of particular importance to the Navajo people.** Not only was the celestial body ingrained in their mythology, but it served a greater utilitarian purpose. Pleiades' progress across the sky throughout the winter months renders it a sort of* *celestial 'clock' for gauging the number of hours until dawn.*

Despite his importance in the act of creation, Black God (or Haashch'eezhini) appears very seldom in Navajo ritual. The only sacrament involving Him is the Nightway (or Yeibichai), a nine-day midwinter healing ceremony. On the ninth and final day of the ritual, a man arrives in the guise of the Black God. It is not uncommon for Black God to be portrayed by an old man dressed in traditional garb including: fox skin, black body paint, and the Black God mask. The impersonator carries with him a fire-drill (a device that uses friction to incite ignition) and shredded bark (tinder) with which he will demonstrate his pyromancy.

There is a conflict between Black God, as the God of Fire, and Begochidi, the creator of birds and animals. This tension originates from the destruction that Black God's fire has wrought on Begochidi's creations. Strangely enough, this rivalry persists despite Black God becoming the protector of said creations in another story. In the story of Deer Raiser, humans have begun to hunt in ways other than those that the gods had ordained. Seeing this, Black God hides game animals inside his home, Black Mountain, and surrounds it with poisonous plants to further ward against intruders.

Source:
https://en.wikipedia.org/wiki/Black_God_(Navajo_mythology)

I am not adding any interpretation to these tales as anyone familiar with the "ancient aliens" lens of history, which I also support, easily understands them. The only people who find these stories "mysterious" are proponents of the fake history of *Scientism.*

Not surprisingly, the Pleiades are also feature prominently in Asia. The semi-nomadic and now nearly extinct Ban Raji or Ban Rawats people of Nepal and Northern India, call them the "seven sisters-in-law and one brother-in-law". When the Pleiades rise up over the mountain each night at around eight o'clock *they feel happy to see their ancient kin*, according to custom. This nicely lines up with my bold claim that the Pleiades are populated by our ancient spacefaring ancestors.

In India, the Pleiades are associated with the fire god Agni and also called the stars of fire. Their god Kartikeya means "him of the Pleiades".

Quoting again from Wikipedia:

Kartikeya, also known as Murugan, Skanda, Kumara, and Subrahmanya, is the Hindu god of war. He is the son of Parvati and Shiva, brother of Ganesha, and a god whose life story has many versions in Hinduism. An important deity around South Asia since ancient times, Kartikeya is particularly popular and predominantly worshipped in South India and Sri Lanka as Murugan.

Kartikeya is an ancient god, traceable to the Vedic era. Archaeological evidence from 1st-century CE and earlier, where he is found with Hindu god Agni (fire), suggest that he was a significant deity in early Hinduism. He is found in many medieval temples all over India, such as at the Ellora Caves and Elephanta Caves.

The iconography of Kartikeya varies significantly; he is typically represented as an ever-youthful man, riding or near a peacock, dressed with weapons sometimes near a rooster. Most icons show him with one head, but some show him with six heads reflecting the legend surrounding his birth where six mothers symbolizing the six stars of Pleiades cluster who took care of newly born baby Kartikeya. He grows up quickly into a philosopher-warrior, destroys evil in the form of demon Taraka, teaches the pursuit of ethical life and the theology of Shaiva Siddhanta.

Across many cultures, the Pleiades are linked to roosters, hens, birds, doves, eagles and other flying creatures. They are also linked to war, for the simple reason that they have been engaged in a war with the Serpent for a very long time.

This is why so many of the ancient warring "gods" are depicted either as dragons (the flying Serpent) or Eagles (the Pleiadean space force). This, for example, is the ancient Egyptian God Horus:

Compare this to the American Eagle (image of a room inside the Federal Reserve Bank):

Have you ever asked yourself why modern and ancient iconography are almost identical? Look closely at the two images above. They are thousands of years apart, but essentially the same. They represent the same sources and forces. However, just because someone displays the symbolism of "the good guys" doesn't necessarily make them trustworthy. That's not the point being made here. The point being made is that none of the symbolism we see being used by world powers, are coincidental and they go back a very long time, and yes, they refer to the ancient war between these two primary extraterrestrial factions.

In Japan, the Pleiades are called "Subaru", meaning "cluster" or "unite". That's why the Japanese car brand Subaru shows the six clearly visible Pleaides on their Logo.

SUBARU

The Japanese Subaru Telescope, stationed at the Mauna Kea Observatory in Hawaii is also named after the Pleiades.

In Thailand, the Pleiades are known as the "Chick Stars", based on another folk tale with positive connotations.

From Wikipedia:

The story tells that a poor elderly couple who lived in a forest had raised a family of chickens: a mother hen and her six (or alternately seven) chicks. One day a monk arrived at the couple's home during his Dhutanga journey. Worried that they had no suitable food to offer him, the elderly couple contemplated cooking the mother hen. The hen overheard the conversation, and rushed back to the coop to say farewell to her children. She told them to take care of themselves, and that her death would repay the kindness of the elderly couple, who had taken care of all of them for so long. As the mother hen's feathers were being burned over a fire, the chicks threw themselves into fire in order to die along with their mother. The deity, impressed by and in remembrance of their love, immortalized the seven chickens as the stars of the Pleiades. In tellings of the story in which there were only six chicks, the mother is included, but often includes only the seven chicks.

And still I have not come across a single negative connotation with the Pleiades. That, in itself, is extraordinary, as normally any topic at all, is subject to duality.

What follows, is an article I found on the internet about the Aborigines of Australia. I have bolded parts of this text that are the most relevant to this research.

"WORLDS' LONGEST LIVING CIVILIZATION SPREADS 65,000 YEAR OLD STORY ABOUT THE CREATION OF STARS

Posted on March 15, 2018 by Inge van Schooneveld

Within the belief system of Aboriginal Australians, a songline, also called dreamtrack, is one of the paths across the land or sky which follow the route taken by so called creator beings during the creation of this world. The paths and landmarks along the way have since been narrated through song, dance and painting. When singing these songlines in appropriate manner and order, the indigenous are capable of navigating along far distances. The continent of Australia harbors a vast network of dreamtracks, some are a few kilometers long while others travers passed hundreds of kilometres through different lands and indigenous communities. Interestingly, since the songline can span the lands of different native language groups, they are often divided into those different languages, so this is not a barrier for them to understand what direction to take, it is rather the rhythm of the song that determines the route, representing an overarching language that connects all the Aboriginal people in Australia. Therefore, both many anthropologists and archeologists are convinced these Dream Tracks are not only significant as land maps or for the transfer of knowledge and local mythology, they are also said to represent prehistoric meaning for (genetic) exchange and communication over long distances.

Take the ***Star Dreaming Story of the Seven Sisters*** *as an example. This story is one of the widest distributed* *amongst ancient songlines of Australia, tracking over half of the continent from the Central Desert up until the west coast. Observed from central Australia, the Pleiades star group rises above the horizon soon after sunset and keeps a low trajectory. Perhaps for this reason,* **such a small star group was given such significance,** *as it appears to launch from the earths' surface right above the land. However, in many ancient traditions, the mythological story of the Pleiades was narrated through the journey of 7 beautiful sisters, each representing one of the constellations' stars. Similar stories of 7 sisters were told in ancient Greece, the Americas and Siberia.*

In the Seven Sisters story of Aboriginal Australia, the group of stars are Napaljarri sisters being chased across land and sky by Jukurra-Jukurra (the morning star), a Jakamarra man in love with the seven sisters, specifically fixated on the oldest sister. When on Martu country, where the seven sisters take humanoid form and live on the ground, they're known as Minyipuru. As they travel further east and decide to fly through the sky to escape their lustful pursuer (and at times avoid country belonging to others), they switch languages and become known as the Kungkarangkalpa. New and gripping episodes in this lengthy saga come into being as the pursuit, escape and journey unfold. Like all Aboriginal creator beings, the man has the capacity to shift shape, transforming himself to lure his 'prey' into coming closer to him. ***In various guises – as an edible snake, or a shady tree, or as temptingly delicious fruit – he devises strategy after strategy to bring the women under his control.*** *But the women too have the ability to change shape and form, so on occasion they become rocks, trees or flowers to avoid his unwanted advances. Although he succeeds once in hoodwinking and brutalising the eldest sister, causing her to become dreadfully ill,* ***ultimately the sisters, in a convincing and intelligent expression of female solidarity, outwit their antagonist.***

Human beings have always looked for a correspondence between micro and macro- cosm in order to find spiritual explanations for natural phenomena and their interpretations often show striking similarities across different times and geographic locations. ***Ancient civilisations of all the world have analogous stories describing the origins of the Pleiades; it seems that different and distant cultures have created similar motives in a similar synchronic way. It seems the Pleiades are the meeting place in the skies of mythology*** *and science and most earth peoples consider them as centres of divine feminine energy.* ***From time immemorial this group of stars is associated with festivities, rites and solemn ceremonies, especially at midnight on 17th November when the Pleiades reach their culmination:*** *in ancient Egypt in honour of Isis; in ancient Persia in that night no petition went unheard; Druids and Celtic Priestesses led midnight rites and auspices, in connection with the midnight rising of the Pleiades; similar to the Aboriginal Dreamtime, in Greek mythology the Pleiades are a group of virgins who flee from Orion the hunter and are akin to the doves of the rock (péleiádes) into which they transformed in order to fly in the sky.*

How is this possible? Establishing links between prehistoric Australia and other parts of the world presents obstacles in the absence of known writing systems. According to Russian palaeohistorian Boris A. Frolov, the gendering and numbering of the Pleiades by the different peoples across time can be explained by there being a system of astronomical knowledge existent before the peopling of Australia and America:

"...mention of the American Indians' observations of the Pleiades, which they called the Seven Sisters, involves an interesting question, for exactly the same name was traditionally used for the Pleiades by the aborigines of both Australia and Siberia, and a similar image of the Pleiades is found in the mythology of ancient Greece. While it seems quite impossible to see in this fact a mere coincidence, there is room for only one supposition: observation of the Pleiades and their denotation by the image of seven sisters pre-dated the populating of America and Australia. In other words, these observations and ideas must have been formed and transmitted by nonliterate Paleolithic hunters"

Frolov articulated his observation about 35 years ago, when the dominant conception held that hunter-gatherers before 10,000 years ago were a brutish, 'primitive' lot outcast from influencing the rise of civilisation. The only astronomical inclination that model would have allowed would have been a wild howling at the moon. But such views are incompatible with the picture painted by new findings today. While some scholars have theorized that indigenous Australians descended from a separate, earlier migration than that of Eurasian people, recent DNA study published by Nature magazine reports that the majority of non-Africans stem from a single ancestral group of migrants who left Africa approximately 72,000 years ago and eventually spread across the other continents. European and Asian ancestral groups became distinct in the genetic record around 42,000 years ago, whilst indigenous Papuan and Australian ancestral groups became genetically distinct 58,000 years ago. Around 50,000 years ago, this wave of migration reached Sahul, a prehistoric supercontinent composed of present-day

Australia, Tasmania and New Guinea prior to their separation by rising sea levels 10,000 years ago. At that time, according to the study's authors, Aboriginal Australians became genetically isolated, making it the world's oldest civilization.

Being the first ones to venture further eastwards, undertaking a very dangerous journey which would've required stamina, these so called primitive hunter-gatherers must have had some knowledge of how to interpret the land and its interrelations. Then is it also impossible to suggest that they were capable of maintaining and spreading 65,000 years old stories about the stars across these continents? Advocate for Frolov's theory and expert in archaeology and ancient religion, writes the following answer in his article 'Denisovan Star Trail: Archaic Memory of the Pleiades in the Worlds' First Story.'

" From a conventional perspective, a 65,000-year period for transportable stories of the stars may appear astounding, far out of sight and before anything we could

relate to as modern humans. The typical argument against such an early transfer of knowledge would be to say that specific stars and constellations could not possibly have retained their identity for such long periods. This, however, would neglect the fact that up until the Younger Dryas event, hunter-gatherer cultures had persisted for millions of years. Given the plummeting time-depth of Australian and American colonisation, and that these early civilisations remained intact within continents that became sealed by oceans until European contact, such a timescale is arguably entirely reasonable."

With that in mind, it is perhaps no coincidence that the flag of Australia features the Pleiades, with six stars and the seventh star being the flags seal itself:

Steven and Evan Strong, experts on the Australian Aborigines, have this to say in an interesting article posted on the internet. The article is about the first humans walking in Australia rather than — as commonly assumed — in Africa. A minor part of the article mentions the Aborigines views on the Pleiades:

If we accept Wilson is correct in identifying Homo erectus (which we do not fully subscribe to but for the sake of balance we will include) as half of the newly emerging Homo sapien sapiens evolutionary model, we need to turn to Original mentors and Elders in discovering the other agency responsible. Whether consulting the Dreaming story " The Seven Sisters " which is spread throughout the continent and is specific in naming the Pleiades as the place from which the sisters came, or seeking the advice of many Elders/ Custodians of Original Lore, there is a continental consistency in the location of the Original ancestry. Reuben Kelly, an incredibly wise and highly respected Dhungutti (Thainghetti) Elder (N.S.W.) was adamant his distant ancestors arrived on this planet on a "space ship". He stated that "our legends tell us that we came to this planet on a space ship made of energy. When it hit this atmosphere, it turned to crystal".

Source: https://www.ancient-origins.net/opinion-guest-authors-human-origins-science/out-africa-yesterday-australia-today-and-pleiades-1

References to the Pleiades continue on into our modern times. For example, the fake religion of the Jehovah's Witnesses, strangely enough, consider Alcyone, the brightest star among the Pleiades, the "throne of God" and officially taught the same prior to the 1950s. How they came about such a doctrine remains unexplained as

I was unable to find further records. But in a strange way it makes sense. In my book *Levels of Energy*, I classified the religion of the Jehovas Witnesses as a "lower vibe" movement as compared to other Christian denominations. Correspondingly, the Pleiades are a "lower vibe" representative of the Highest Realms.

In Theosophy, the predecessor of the modern New Age movement, it is said that the Seven Stars of the Pleiades focus seven rays of energy from the Galactic Center and Sirius to the Sun, then to the "God of Earth" Sanat Kumara and finally through the "seven Ascended Masters of the Seven Rays" to us. I don't know how theosophists and came to such beliefs as I do not resonate with Theosophy enough to have studied it.

In my own Pleiadean event, described at the beginning of this book, an image was transmitted to me that I did not fully understand. While it differs somewhat from the description given by Theosophists, there are vague similarities. I do not know what the image means, but I have made sure to reproduce it for this book. I believe it to mean that "Source Energy" travels to us through various filters. The image I received is this:

It could also mean that our own path of ascension follows this trail:

First we achieve the consciousness level of the Pleiades, then of Sirius, then Galactic Consciousness and finally the Enlightenment of the Infinite Field. Incidentally, after creating this image in my photoshop program, I found other, similar Theosophy-inspired images floating around the internet. So either both I and the Theosophists received the same information, or I received my transmission from Theosophists trying to remote brainwash me into their worldview (hopefully not! :-)).

My focus throughout life, however, has not been the Pleiades, it has been the "Field" and the "Highest Source". If you aim for the stars, you'll at least reach the moon. And if this depiction represents a model of ascension, then aiming for the Field will have me at least reach the Pleiades. At least that's my best guess. With all due respect toward my research and experience, I do not want readers to take my writings as religion or absolute, but rather as possibilities and areas that require further research. In fact, I wish nobody would ever stop researching and learning. If I were to say that the depicted path of ascension is "the truth" or "the way things are", that would close peoples' minds toward looking further and more deeply. The same applies to all other models of reality.

What I do know is that the Blue Beings I encountered say that they are both from Sirius and from the Pleiades. The Blue Beings manifest at two different levels of consciousness. On Sirius, they're mostly non-physical and on the Pleiades, they are semi-physical. Why they descended, I do not know. It could have something to do with complacency, which I know to be one of the challenges of that level.

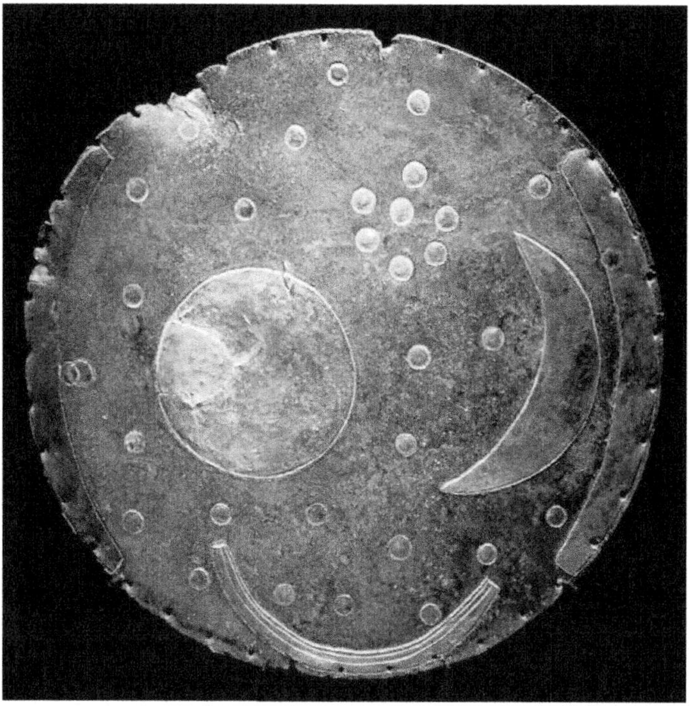

The image above has been called the "Nebra Sky Disk".

The Nebra sky disk is a bronze disk of around 30 centimeters (12 in) diameter and a weight of 2.2 kilograms (4.9 lb), with a blue-green patina and inlaid with gold symbols. These are interpreted generally as a sun or full moon, a lunar crescent, and stars (including a cluster interpreted as the Pleiades). Two golden arcs along the sides, marking the angle between the solstices, were added later. A final addition was another arc at the bottom surrounded with multiple strokes (of uncertain meaning, variously interpreted as a Solar Barge with numerous oars, as the Milky Way, or as a rainbow).

The disk is attributed to a site near Nebra, Saxony-Anhalt, in Germany, and associatively dated to c. 1600 BC. It has been associated with the Bronze Age Unetice culture.

The disk is unlike any known artistic style from the period, and was initially suspected of being a forgery, but now is widely accepted as authentic.

The Nebra sky disk features the oldest concrete depiction of the cosmos worldwide. In June 2013 it was included in the UNESCO Memory of the World Register and termed "one of the most important archaeological finds of the twentieth century."

You can read more on it here:

https://en.wikipedia.org/wiki/Nebra_sky_disk

What makes this object worthy of inclusion is that it shows how people as far back as 1600 B.C. were keenly aware of the importance of the Pleiades. At first the authenticity of the object was attacked by Archaeologists because some still maintain that people of that period and area not have any reliable astronomical knowledge. It is now, fortunately, widely acknowledged to be authentic.

Yet another ancient culture that explicitly referred to the Pleiades as the "seabed of civilization" were the Mayans. In their mythology they say that the "cosmic mother" from who they received "codes of light" came from the Pleiades. Mayan writings, of course, speak extensively of the wars of serpents with other beings, as already described in detail elsewhere.

The Serpent vs. the Bird in Buddhism and Hinduism

This same war is described in every other culture. For example, according to ancient Buddhist and Hindu literature, the enemies of enlightenment are the Naga, a type of the Serpent creature. I like Buddhist sources of information as they have proven fairly reliable throughout thirty years of research.

Quoting again from Wikipedia:

The mythological ***serpent race*** *that took form as cobras often can be found in Hindu iconography. The nāgas are described as the powerful, splendid, wonderful and proud* ***semidivine*** *race that can* ***assume their physical form*** *either as human, partial human-serpent or the whole serpent. Their domain is in the enchanted* ***underworld****, the* ***underground*** *realm filled with gems, gold and other earthly treasures called Naga-loka or Patala-loka. They are also often associated with bodies of waters — including rivers, lakes, seas, and wells — and are guardians of treasure. Their power and venom made them potentially dangerous to humans. However, they often took beneficial protagonist role in Hindu mythology, such as in Samudra manthan mythology, Vasuki, a nāgarāja who abides on Shiva's neck, became the churning rope for churning of the* ***Ocean of Milk****.*

Their eternal mortal enemies are the Garudas, the legendary semidivine ***birdlike****-deity.*

Allow me to translate this into my words: "semi divine" refers to their fallen state of no longer being in the spiritual realm and yet having memories and powers higher than those of Earth-dwelling humans. The reference "assuming physical form" means they are astral beings that can manifest physically. Being "underground" and "underworld" refers to the interior of Earth. All ancient "myths" from around the globe that reference "the underworld" refer to inner Earth as well as the lower astral realm which is connected to it. Mainstream anthropologists claim that the underworld refers to "the afterlife", but I'd strongly suggest that is *not* the afterlife most readers want to visit. The "ocean of milk" refers to the Milky Way, pointing out the fact that the Nagas are a space-faring race. Their enemy being a "birdlike" deity is a reference to the Pleiades, which are referred to with bird symbols throughout the world.

The Pleiadeans too are "semi divine" (albeit at a higher consciousness level) in that they do not occupy Sirian, Galactic or Field Consciousness but "merely" Pleiadean Consciousness. Earth-dwellers are one step lower in that we have not yet achieved the consciousness level of the Pleiadeans but have also not descended to the lower astral realms. We are at a point in between the two and have this Earth-life to decide whether we go up or down.

The Buddhist nāga generally has the form of a great cobra, usually with a single head but sometimes with many. At least ***some of the nāgas are capable of using magic powers to transform themselves into a human semblance.*** *In Buddhist painting, the nāga is sometimes portrayed as a human being with a snake or dragon extending over his head. One nāga, in human form, attempted to become a monk; and when telling it that such ordination was impossible, the Buddha told it how to ensure that it would be reborn a human, and so able to become a monk.*

From what I saw, it is true that "some Nagas" are able to become physical or even appear as human. Many of them (approximately 90%) are now bound to the astral. It is also accurate that they can ascend in consciousness, if they so choose, and leave their astral realm. This important fact is not mentioned in Abrahamic religions that speak of "eternal" hell for the fallen ones. A being of exceptionally high consciousness, such as the Buddha, would not only know this fact but be able to help and facilitate such a transition. In a loving universe, no punishment is forever and there is always a chance to move upward.

The doctrine of "Eternal Hell" is a sadistic teaching that is not native to Christianity but taught as such in its modern form. In the first five centuries that doctrine was not known among Christians. It was only introduced later, by Romans and borrowed from pagan beliefs about the fiery depths of hell that one is trapped in "for ever and ever". In the Bible, the words "for ever and ever" are translated from the word "Aeon". The problem is, that the word "Aeon" doesn't mean forever, it means "age".

So what the Bible actually teaches is that spirits are locked in an unpleasant place for a certain *age*, not eternally. And yet, modern "Christianity" keeps claiming that punishment is "eternal", which really doesn't make any sense at all. If I am burning for ten trillion years in "hellfire" what is the point of being punished another ten trillion years and then another, for eternity? In any case, Buddhist scripts portray other realms more accurately.

In the "Devadatta" chapter of the Lotus Sutra, the daughter of the dragon king, an eight year old longnü (nāga), after listening to Mañjuśrī preach the Lotus Sutra, transforms into a male Bodhisattva and immediately reaches full enlightenment...

Nagas are believed to both live on Mount Meru, among the other minor deities, and in various parts of the human-inhabited earth. Some of them are water-dwellers, living in streams or the ocean; ***others are earth-dwellers, living in underground caverns.***

Source: https://en.wikipedia.org/wiki/Naga

What is unmentioned in the Wikipedia entry, is that the Nagas are considered *enemies* of enlightenment (spiritual liberation) in some Buddhist literature. Other Buddhist and Hindu literature refers to them as friends of humankind. Their overall role is more foggy in these Religions, whereas in Abrahamic religions they are clearly designated as the "bad guys". The article cites examples of them being worshipped and coming to the help and rescue of Buddha. This could be the Serpent propaganda, not unlike that encountered by the Shamanic Ayahuasca account quoted earlier. Hence, Asian culture reveres them in countless statues, etchings, murals and paintings. On the other hand, some of the Serpent actually *are* friendly towards humans, so it's hard to say who's who.

There is a Buddhist story that recounts how a Naga wished to become a monk to achieve enlightenment. The Buddha told him that he could not become enlightened yet taught him how to be reborn as a human being, by which he could then open the possibility for enlightenment.

Another internet source has this to say (commentary mine):

Nagas belonged to half animal and half god realm.

The Sanskrit word naga means snake or serpent. Nagas belong half to the animal realm and half to the god realm.

The Serpent is the offspring of mixing Divine Consciousness with animal consciousness. Hence, they have semi-divine powers but the ruthless mentality of animals. This is what makes them "the bad guys" or the "enemy" of mankind. But, seen from a less judgmental perspective, a more Buddhist one perhaps, they are merely fulfilling their role as the polar opposite of good.

Nagas are often snake-like in form, creatures with the torso and head of humans, and the body and tail of a snake, though they can assume human form at will.

At the time that this was written, they were able to assume human form at will. From what I know, this is no longer true.

They dwell in a variety of locations ranging from waterways and underground locations and also in unseen realms.

These are the unseen astral realms. Nowadays even more than in the times this was written. Because they have been losing the interstellar and intergalactic war with the Pleiadeans, they are increasingly confined to the astral.

They are broadly divided into two classes: those that live on land (thalaja) and those that live on water (jalaja). The Jalaja-naga live in rivers as well as in the sea, while the Thalaja-naga are regarded as living beneath the surface of the earth.

Nagas have their own society and kingdoms under the earth and are often the custodian of treasures: either texts or actual material treasures underground.

From what I know, this is true. The treasures they are custodians of, include the spoils of war from various planets, remnants from Atlantis, as well as precious metals they themselves mined. In the physical realm, their material wealth far exceeds anything imaginable to us Earthlings. The combined wealth of human beings is approximately 300 trillion, according to economists. From their perspective, 300 trillion is peanuts, like three cents is to us. Some of the subterranean treasures are either unattended or abandoned (they don't mind losing three cents), so any adventurer who'd venture deep, could find gems and precious metals that would make them richer than anyone on the planet. But people usually do not make it out alive. The terrain is dangerous and the creatures are deadly. Yes, many have ventured underground to try to find lost kingdoms and hidden treasures. In fact, the Nazis spent a lot of time and money sending expeditions to the interior of Earth, through the Himalayas, the Antarctica and other locations. As far as I know, all of their expeditions were unsuccessful. After Nazi-Germany fell, the Russians and Americans continued to explore and venture underground. I am not sure what transpired from these searches, as these activities are non-public.

Some are infinitely wealthy and owe their present form to a previous life of unethical generosity.

"Unethical generosity" is a term frequently used to describe the mentality or path of the Naga. It is said that this is "their Karma". Unethical generosity refers to the practice of giving and expecting in return or giving with strings attached. It is the basis of money lending with interest or letting someone be rich and famous with preconditions, obligations and clauses. In our culture this is called "selling your soul to the devil".

Their lives are long and they are gifted with miraculous powers and great strength. Nagas are easily angered and passionate.

One of the complaints the Serpent have about higher consciousness beings is that they lack passion, sense of romance, sexuality, poetry or artistic sense. That they are too neutral and calm. They claim that their influence on humankind is what makes humans live worthwhile — a life of passion, zest and fire.

On this point, I actually agree with their serpent-wisdom to a certain degree. Humans do need a little bit of fire to enjoy life. Always being calm, neutral, civilized, restrained and disciplined, makes for a peaceful but uneventful life. The downside of this philosophy: Too much fire is destructive. A little bit of fire is warming. So yes, it is good to have passion, poetry, romance, sexuality in your life. It is good to be adventurous and daring. It is good to be poetic and emotional. But when fire becomes the main focus and basis of your life, it eventually turns destructive. Fire needs to be controlled and not allowed to be spread uncontrollably. The result of exaggerated "passion" is rage, hate, war, rape and murder, which run counter to the survival of humankind.

Nagas are susceptible to suffering created by mankind's carelessness and basic ignorance of proper conduct in nature and disrespectful actions in relation to our environment. The weaker nagas will undergo great hardship or die off, while the more powerful will react with anger and strike back at the offenders, inflicting skin diseases, death, and sudden catastrophe like floods and drought. Additionally, Nagas can bestow various types of wealth, bring rain and thus assure fertility of crops and the environment as well as decline these blessings. For this reason, the practice of Lu Sang (offering of smoke) can be performed as a method to increase prosperity, and assist the Nagas by preserving the positive qualities of their natural environment.

While the Serpent are often negative and deceptive about some things, they can also be quite sincere about others. Environmental protection is one of them. While I do support respecting the environment to a degree, I would not support making offerings to the Serpent, nor communicating with them, making deals with them, etc. Their path is radically different than that of humankind and they have nothing of lasting value to offer us. They do not care about humans and involvement with them is the opposite of involvement with the Universe's Highest Source.

Quoting from Wikipedia on the "mortal enemy" of the Serpent, the Garuda (pay attention, because this is stuff they did not teach you in history class. By labeling our history as "myth" it was removed from collective memory):

The Garuda is a legendary bird or bird-like creature in Hindu, Buddhist and Jain mythology. He is variously the vehicle mount (vahana) of the Hindu god Vishnu, a dharma-protector and Astasena in Buddhism, and the Yaksha of the Jain Tirthankara Shantinatha.

Garuda is described as the king of birds and a kite-like figure. He is shown either in zoomorphic form (giant bird with partially open wings) or an anthropomorphic form (man with wings and some bird features). Garuda is generally a protector with power to swiftly go anywhere, ever watchful and an enemy of the serpent. He is also known as Tarkshya and Vynateya.

In Hinduism, Garuda is a divine eagle-like sun bird and the king of birds. A Garutman is mentioned in the Rigveda who is described as celestial deva with wings.The Shatapatha Brahmana embedded inside the Yajurveda text mentions Garuda as the personification of courage. In the Mahabharata, Garutman is stated to be same as Garuda, then described as the one who is fast, who can shapeshift into any form and enter anywhere.

He is a powerful creature in the epics, whose wing flapping can stop the spinning of heaven, earth and hell. He is described to be the vehicle mount of the Hindu god Vishnu, and typically they are shown together.

...

According to the text Silparatna, states Rao, Garuda is best depicted with only two hands and with four bands of colors: "golden yellow color from feet to knees, white from knees to navel, scarlet from navel to neck, and black above the neck". His hands, recommends the text, should be in abhaya (nothing to fear) posture.

Garuda mythology is linked to that of Aruna – the charioteer of Surya (Sun god).

Some myths present Garuda as so massive that he can block out the sun.

Garuda's links to Vishnu – the Hindu god who fights injustice and destroys evil in his various avatars to preserve dharma, has made him an iconic symbol of king's duty and power, an insignia of royalty or dharma.

His eagle-like form is shown either alone or with Vishnu, signifying divine approval of the power of the state. He is found on the faces of many early Hindu kingdom coins with this symbolism, either as a single headed bird or a three-headed bird that watches all sides.

Throughout the Mahabharata, Garuda is invoked as a symbol of impetuous violent force, of speed, and of martial prowess. Powerful warriors advancing rapidly on doomed foes are likened to Garuda swooping down on a serpent. Defeated warriors are like snakes beaten down by Garuda. The Mahabharata character Drona uses a military formation named after Garuda. Krishna even carries the image of Garuda on his banner.

Garuda, also referred to as Garula (Pali), are golden-winged birds in Buddhist texts. Under the Buddhist concept of saṃsāra, they are one of the Aṣṭagatyaḥ, the eight classes of inhuman beings. In Buddhist arts, they are shown as sitting and listening to the sermons of the Buddha. They are enemies of Nagas (snakes) and therefore sometimes depicted with a serpent held between their claws. Like the Hindu arts, both zoomorphic (giant eagle-like bird) and partially anthropomorphic (part bird, part human) iconography has been common in Buddhism.

In Buddhism, the Garuda (Pāli: garuḷā) are enormous predatory birds with wings span of 330 yojanas. They are described as beings with intelligence and social organization. Another name for the Garuda is suparṇa (Pāli: supaṇṇa), meaning "well-winged, having good wings". Like the Naga, they combine the characteristics of animals and divine beings, and may be considered to be among the lowest devas. The Garudas have kings and cities, and at least some of them have the magical power of changing into human form when they wish to have dealings with people. On some occasions Garuda kings have had romances with human women in this form. …

Jataka stories describe them to be residents of Nagadipa. …

The Garuda are enemies to the nāga, a race of intelligent serpent- or dragon-like beings, whom they hunt. …

The Garudas were among the beings appointed by Śakra to guard Mount Sumeru and the Trāyastriṃśa heaven from the attacks of the asuras.

In the Maha-samaya Sutta (Digha Nikaya 20), the Buddha is shown making temporary peace between the Nagas and the Garudas.

Source: https://en.wikipedia.org/wiki/Garuda

Ancient scripture even tells us where the Garuda had one of their military bases, in a place called "Nagadip", which is today a small Island of Sri Lanka and location to one of the most revered sites of Buddhism.

If my idea is correct and the Garuda are Pleiadeans, then we should *easily* find evidence for the assertion. Let's begin with the Hindu name for the Pleiades: Kṛttikā.

Wikipedia has this to say:

In Hindu astrology, Kṛttikā is the third of the 27 nakṣatras. It is ruled by Sun.

Source: https://en.wikipedia.org/wiki/ Kṛttikā

As the Garuda are said to represent the sun, it follows that the Garuda rule the Pleiades. See? It's that easy.

Hindu depictions of Garuda:

Here is a common Hindu myth about the Krttika (commentary mine):

In the Hindu mythology, it is said that the stars of the Big Dipper were the seven sages called Rishis. They were happily married to seven sisters named Krttika. They originally lived all together in the northern sky. But one day, the god of fire, Agni, emerged from the flames of a sacrificial offering performed by the seven Rishis and immediately fell in love with the seven Krttika.

Trying to forget his love for the Krttika, Agni wandered in the forest where he met Svaha, the star Zeta Tauri. Svaha fell in love with Agni. To conquer Agni's love, Svaha disguised herself as six of the seven Krttika. For six times, Svaha made love to Agni, who believed that he had conquered the attractive wives of the seven Rishis.

Svaha could mimic only six of the Krttika since the seventh sister, Arundhati, was too devoted to her husband to be imitated. After a while, Svaha gave birth to a child that she named Skanda. With his birth, rumors began to spread that six of the Rishis' wives were his mother.

The seven Rishis divorced their wives. Arundhati was the only one that remained with her husband as the star Alcor. The other six Krttika went away to become the Pleiades.

Source:

https://www.windows2universe.org/mythology/krttika_pleiades.html&edu=high

While I do not know the exact meaning of this story, it is interesting that the six visible Pleiades are again associated with some kind of fall from Grace whereas the seventh star represents maintained purity.

The Mystical Number Seven

The importance of the Pleiades is globally encoded in the number seven. In several very ancient traditions it is said that the whole of existence is contained in seven areas, seven universes, seven dimensions. It is, therefore, perhaps no coincidence that the number eight is also the symbol of ∞ infinity, which transcends the whole of creation. Seven being the "blueprint of creation" it would then follow that this number is encoded in various subjects that are related to our origins. And so it is…

According to particular schools of Vedic thought, human life itself, or our physical makeup, originates in a system of "seven stars". This is echoed in various ancient tribal mythologies of Africa and Asia which also make reference to the "seven stars" as our "home". It is quite possible that they are talking of the Pleiades and that extraterrestrial Pleiadeans played a part in the creation of our bodies.

As a reminder of our origin we have seven chakras (energy-systems) in our bodies. The chakras regulate the flow of life energy and it is at their specific points we feel emotion most strongly. An interesting analogy to this are the "seven emotional states" and the corresponding "Sephirot" referred to in the Kabbalah.

Because Hinduism refers to there being "seven universes" in all of creation, the number traverses many of India's rituals and traditions. For instance, a Hindu who marries must make "seven vows" to their partner.

The significance of the number seven is encoded in *every* world religion, as if it is a signal whereby to recognize divine origins. In Islam there are seven heavens, seven hells and seven layers of Earth (as shown in my book *Journeys in Spectral Consciousness* these layers correspond to Levels of Consciousness). There are seven gates to hell and eight gates to heaven (which makes sense if eight is seen as infinity). There are seven counter-clockwise circumambulations made around Muslims most sacred site, the Kaaba.

In Judaism, seven is considered "the number of God". There were seven days of creation in the book of Genesis. The week has seven days. The Passover feast is seven days. The Menorah has seven branches. There are "seven pillars in the house of wisdom". A Jewish bride and groom receive seven blessings. There are many, many more references to the number seven in the Old Testament, too many to bring up here.

Want to learn something interesting? In Hebrew seven is pronounced "Shiva". In Hinduism Shiva is sometimes referred to as the "God with seven faces". Perhaps there is more of a connection between the *Brahmic* (Hindu) and *Abrahamic* (Judaism, Christianity, Islam) religions than commonly known and maybe "Brahma" and "Abraham" refer to the same source.

The Menorah of seven candles is a sacred object found in Jewish Synagogues and Temples:

According to the historian Josephus Flavius, these seven lights represent "the seven celestial bodies". Researchers have suggested that these seven celestial bodies are the Pleiades and that the seven Christian candles placed on the altar mirror the same idea. Some even go so far as to say that the Christian cross is meant to depict the layout of these seven stars as seen from Earth.

In the Kabbalah (Jewish Mysticism), the Tree of Life contains seven energy or emotional centers (and an additional four levels of higher consciousness). This is mirrored in the seven chakras of Hinduism.

Christianity is also pervaded by the seven. The New Testament refers to those who sin being forgiven seven times. At one time Jesus recommends to forgive a person seven times seventy. Jesus multiplied seven loaves of bread into seven baskets full of bread. When he was on the cross he spoke seven last sayings. The Book of Revelations refers to the “Seven Seals”, “Seven Spirits of God”, “Seven Churches”, “Seven Stars”, “Seven Horns”, “Seven Torches”, “Seven Angels”, “Seven Kings”, “Seven Trumpets”, “Seven Heads of the Beast”, “Seven Spirits of God” among other things. Christianity teaches of the seven deadly sins and the seven virtues. Catholicism has numerous additional sevens, such as the Seven Sacraments, the Seven Corporeal Acts of Mercy, the Seven Spiritual Acts of Mercy, Seven Joys of Virgin Mary, etc.

Seven is also encoded outside of the world religions. Ancient mythologies refer to “seven sisters”, “seven archangels”, “seven divine women” having founded the world. Japanese mythology speaks of the “seven Gods of good fortune”. When Buddha was born he “walked seven steps” as if to announce to the world that he belongs to divine lineage. Even Plato uses the code of seven in saying that Atlantis consisted of seven islands.

A musical scale has seven notes. There are seven liberal arts. There are seven basic colors in the spectrum. The human head has seven features, plants of pure strain, such as the Lotus, have seven petals, the ziggurat (latter to heaven) has seven steps, there are the “seven kings of Rome”, there were “seven sages of Greece” and seven wonders of the ancient world. The Statue of Liberty has seven rays. The world's oceans are called "the seven seas". In many languages, when you are feeling very good you say, "I`m in 7th Heaven". A human life goes through seven stages or ages. There are seven Hermetic principles, which are as follows:

1. The Law of Mentalism
2. The Law of Correspondence
3. The Law of Vibration
4. The Law of Polarity
5. The Law of Rhythm
6. The Law of Cause and Effect
7. The Law of Gender

The list just goes on and on, but I think by now you get the point: Every time a reference is made to the origins or building blocks of life or some divine origin, the number seven is used. Like the ancients say, seven is the number of completion and perfection of the physical universe. It represents the physical universe as it is meant to be when the work is done (on the 7th Day).

But of what use could this arcane knowledge be for you personally, if any? Well, you could summon the number anytime you require divine intervention or guidance, have something very important to communicate or to take care of. You can use it with the idea that it is some kind of mystical code that will give your endeavors a "divine boost".

Here are seven examples of how I have used the number:

- Felt discouraged and wrote down seven encouraging actions to take.
- Felt resentment, forgave the person seven times.
- Had a special intention, repeated it exactly seven times.
- Gave myself seven times seven (49) days to establish a new habit.

- Reduced my to-do-lists to "no more than seven items" (a priority-list of twenty items is not a *priority*-list!)

- Learned a foreign language and repeated each lesson seven times.

- Had a long lecture to give and repeated my main point seven times throughout the speech so that it was remembered.

Another way of approaching this is by noticing the occurrence of seven in daily life and using it as a sort of "omen", "pointer" or "synchronicity" of good fortune. When you define one number as your "lucky number", you imprint the field of consciousness with that, and it will use that number to communicate with you in daily life. The last five addresses I lived at all had the house number five. I only discovered this recently, when remembering my last addresses. The fact that all of my addresses were at number five is mind-boggling. So why that number? Because I had, when I was young, defined it as my "lucky number". If some book claims that the number eleven is really deep and meaningful, you will start seeing 11s everywhere and using that as "communication from the Universe". And to some extent, that will work. While writing this book, I now live at an address that adds up to seven.

But because the number seven appears to be a genuine "divine number", having been mentioned all around the globe and being the very blueprint of life, why not define it as your "lucky number"?

Interestingly, all major cities have been or at one time have been claimed to be built upon seven hills. Rome was intentionally laid out on seven hills and these hills appear to reflect the layout of the Pleiadean star map. Other cities built or claimed to have been built on seven hills include: Jerusalem, The Holy City and site of three world religions. Mecca, the focal point of Islam. Athens, the birthplace of Politics. Macau, Budapest, Liverpool, Lisbon, Kottayam, Tehran, Istanbul, Moscow, Kampala, Melbourne, Sydney, Asuncion, San Francisco, Mumbai, Kiev, Brussels, Edinburgh, Bergen, Barcelona, Sheffield,

Seattle, Amman, Trivandrum, Prague and others. A more complete list can be found online with a simple search query.

The Nature of the Blue Beings

Having had the origin and nature of the Blue Beings revealed to me, I ventured online, using search engines to learn anything I could about them. Unfortunately, the "knowledge" about aliens on thousands of websites, is abysmal. There are so many contradictions and made-up stories that it becomes pointless to try to discern genuine knowledge from nonsense. Some of the knowledge on Pleiadeans appears to contain certain truths to appeal to our intuitive knowledge, mixed with false information to lead astray. Ancient accounts of blue-skinned beings proved more coherent.

First off, it turns out that whenever the "ancient gods" were depicted as something other than reptiles, they were almost always shown to have either human skin or blue skin. This is an ancient depiction of Lord Krishna:

Interestingly, if Krishna is shown as any other skin color, it is not white but black. Some traditional writings describe him as a "black God", some as a "blue God".

The reason this is interesting to me personally, is because the Pleiadeans I originally encountered as a child all had Negroid features. It is therefore possible that the Blue Pleiadeans have some kind of forgotten relationship to the black African ethnicity. If that were true (and I am not sure it is), that would make the African Continent the enemy to the secret rulers of this Planet – the Serpent. What is true, however, is that some Native American legends speak of "The Black God" when referring to the Pleiades.

From what I can ascertain, the Blue-Skinned beings are originally from Sirius, occupying part of the Pleiades and the Human-Skinned Beings (the Garuda) are originally from Earth and occupying another part of the Pleiades.

For reasons unknown to both myself and many scholars it appears, a number of Ancient Egyptian Gods were portrayed as blue-skinned. This is the "God" Tatanen:

And this is the "God" Amun:

This is Akshobhya, one of the Five Aspects of Buddha, who is almost always depicted as blue-skinned:

From Wikipedia (bolding mine):

In Vajrayana Buddhism, Akshobhya (Sanskrit: अक्षोभ्य, Akṣobhya, "Immovable One"; simplified Chinese and Japanese: 阿閦如来; pinyin: Āchùrúlái;) is one of the

Five Wisdom Buddhas, a product of the Adibuddha, who represents consciousness as an aspect of reality. By convention he is located in the east of the ***Diamond Realm and is the lord of the Eastern Pure Land Abhirati ('The Joyous')****, although the Pure Land of Akshobhya's western counterpart Amitābha is far better known. His consort is Lochanā and he is normally accompanied by two elephants. His color is blue-black and his attributes include the bell, three robes, and staff, along with a jewel, lotus, prayer wheel, and sword. He has several emanations.*

Source: https://en.wikipedia.org/wiki/Akshobhya

This is of interest to me because "The Pure Land" is not the highest level of enlightenment attainable, but rather a joyous pre-state to the Infinite, which would nicely align with what I said earlier about the Pleiades being just one stage to the highest level of "The Field".

In Hindu Astrology, the Pleiades are associated with Rajas-Rajas-Sattva. If you have read my book *Levels of Energy*, you know that this is a reasonably high level of consciousness, but by no means enlightened as there is only one component of "Sattva" and two components of Raja. Hence, the white-skinned Pleiadean God Agni is called the "Lord of War". The Pleiadeans are mainly known for their wars against the Serpent and for publishing anti-serpent propaganda in the form of our world religions. If they were enlightened, they would not be engaged in waging war. In fact, Hinduism considers Pleiadeans "fallen Devas" (fallen angels), just like the Serpent. I mention this as not to give the impression that the "good guys" are completely innocent.

I know next to nothing about the Yazidi religion of Armenia, but add notes on it here in case it is relevant. The following is an image of the primary angel or object of worship of that religion, called "Melek Taus":

I drew this from Wikipedia (bolding mine):

Melek Taus (Ezdiki: Tawûsê Melek), also spelled Malik Tous, translated in English as ***Peacock Angel,*** *is one of the central figures of Yazidi religion. In Yazidi creation stories,* ***God created the world and entrusted it to the care of seven Holy Beings, often known as Angels or heft sirr ('the Seven Mysteries'),*** *preeminent of which is Tawûsê Melek, the Peacock Angel.*

The Yazidi consider Tawûsê Melek an emanation of God and a good, benevolent angel who has redeemed himself from his fall and has become a demiurge who created the cosmos from the Cosmic egg. After he repented, he wept for 7,000 years, his tears filling seven jars, which then quenched the fires of hell. Yazidis believe Tawûsê Melek is not a source of evil or wickedness. They consider him to be the leader of the archangels, not a still-fallen nor a still-disgraced angel, but a forgiven one and an emanation of God himself. They also hold that the source of evil is in the heart and spirit of humans themselves, not in Tawûsê Melek. Yazidis believe that good and evil both exist in the mind and spirit of human beings. It depends on the humans, themselves, as to which they choose. In this process, their devotion to Tawûsê Melek is essential, since it was he who was given the same choice between good and evil by God, and chose the good.

Source: https://en.wikipedia.org/wiki/Melek_Taus

It is likely no coincidence that their primary angel is linked to a bird as well as the blue skin color or that this Blue Being is given rulership of "seven angels". It might be an attempt by a Pleiadean on religion-creating. Or perhaps multiple religions are the creation of extraterrestrials. I don't know.

Most recently, the Yazidi of Armenia have suffered genocide at the hands of the ISIS armies that reigned between 2013 and 2017. Ironically, ISIS have accused the Yazidi of being "Satan worshippers". I don't think that the genocidal ISIS troops are a reliable source of spiritual advice. But it is interesting that the Yazidis believe that Melek Taus is a "redeemed" fallen angel.

All in all, while interesting, none of this online browsing about the "Blue Beings" came close to my *experiential* understanding of them. I am not all that interested in the historical items, I merely add them for reference and documentary support. And I have even less interest in worshipping or revering anyone just because they happen to be from another planet.

What I know, or what was communicated to me, is that the Blue Beings lived around the Pleiades long before our human ancestors arrived there. They descended from the "Sirius" Level of Being, but some of them still reside on Sirius. And some actually travel back and forth between the two. From the viewpoint of astronomy, this doesn't make sense, as Sirius is merely one star just like one of the stars of the Pleiades. But metaphysically speaking, these areas carry a different vibratory frequency.

Travelling between vibratory frequencies is an amazing experience that's hard to describe. Depending on whether you are travelling upwards or downwards its either intensely pleasant or smothering unpleasantness. We do shift vibratory frequency on Earth, but only by a few levels on any given day. So I might be at around 400 in the morning and drop to 380 by evening. But the shifts we are talking about here are several thousand levels per trip. That's why there are what could be called "adaption stations" in between the Pleiades and Sirius, in which one can slowly adapt to the change of vibration if one chooses to. Perhaps you have visited a sauna or hot springs before, where you go from very hot water or cabin to very cold water of ice bucket several times. And while you know that the shift can be incredibly unpleasant, you eventually get used to it. In fact, the more you go back and forth, the more you transcend the duality and relax. The trip between Pleiades and Sirius is similar. When you go down one density (say, a thousand levels) it feels like you are being constricted and tightened into a heavy, suffocating realm. When you move upward, it feels like you just became much lighter and happier. That's one of the reasons Pleiadean humans are not too keen on manifesting on Planet Earth. The Blue Sirians that descended to the Pleiades did so very slowly, almost unnoticeably.

The Blue Beings are serene and playful. They require the assistance of Human Pleiadeans for strategic defense and warfare. At their consciousness level, they have no interest in war of any sort and let the Human Pleiadeans do that kind of work for them. Referring back to my "Levels of Energy" scale from previous books, the average consciousness level of Blue Sirians could be said to be 3000, that of the Blue Pleiadeans 1000 and that of Human Pleiadeans between 500 and 1000. It is higher for those Human Pleiadeans that do not engage in warfare but stay behind on their Planets. War usually has a detrimental effect on consciousness levels. The average level of Earth Consciousness lingers at around 200. In exchange for defense, they share their blissfully pleasant state of consciousness with the Human Pleiadeans.

Some of them have lived among humans as teachers. Krishna appears to have been one of them and his peaceful teachings still echo down to this day. Of course, Hinduism has, just like all other religions, become polluted and diverted by endless distractions, but in its core, it was peaceful because it originated with Krishna. Interestingly, Indian culture actually shares a few of the shortcomings that the Blue Pleiadeans have. Their peaceful nature has manifested as passivity, allowing them to easily be exploited by more negative agendas, which lie at the root of their poverty. Perhaps peaceful people require a more aggressive people for protection like sheep require dogs. In fact, the Blue Pleiadeans did not require protection while they existed one octave higher, at Sirius. But having descended to the denser and more physical Pleiadean plane, they became vulnerable to outside attacks. It was the Blue Pleiadeans that inwardly *called for* fleets of humans to settle in their star system. After their own solar system and Mars had been destroyed, countless fleets of human starships roamed the Galaxy, many of them without fixed destination. It was in this undecided state that they were receptive to the telepathic beckoning of the Pleiades.

The density of humans allows them to engage in military activity. Of course, from our Earthling perspective, the Human Pleiadeans are of a higher consciousness and you might be wondering how it is that a higher consciousness than ours still engages in military violence. But the next higher level is not a perfect world. There are still conflicts, there is still crime, there is still tragedy and drama. At an average consciousness level of 750, they may still experience pockets of the 200s for instance. Of course, crime is minimal. And warfare is only waged against one singular enemy — the Serpent, not against any other. It is also waged defensively, never as an attack, never pre-emptively or provocatively, but always to protect the peaceful. This is comparable to a dog who only jumps into action when the flock of sheep are being attacked by wolves. While not perfect, Pleiadean society would seem magical to us if we were to visit there. It is not that different from Planet Earth, except that everything is more sparkling, happier, clearer, purer, more advanced, more amazing.

Because my Earth-Self likes playing tennis, I was sent a transmission regarding a similar ballgame on one of the planets of the Pleiades. The game was played on a floating field that consisted of some type of stable energy platform. The field was about five times larger than ours. But the players wore especially designed suits that allowed them to sprint much more quickly in order to traverse the large field. This suit also protected against the "ball" which was, again, an "energy ball" that could kill if the suits weren't worn. The ball travelled more quickly than ours and when it flew out of bounds it was replaced by a new manifestation of a ball that appeared on something akin to "rackets". However, these "rackets" or devices with which to strike the ball, were built into the suit the players were wearing. And rather than looking like a tennis racket, it looked more like a light-sword. The "ball" being made of a type of energy, it made the most delightful sounds when it was hit or swooshed through the air. When it hit the racket, the net or the ground, it let of sparks. Professional matches might be watched by trillions of people from around the star system in addition to a crowd of millions present around the field. Due to the speed of the ball and size of the field, it had a squash element to it in that one can target one of the invisible walls surrounding the field to have the ball ricochet off of it and into the opponent's field. And with enough grit, a player was able to jump higher than a normal body could. It was almost like flying. Whether this was due to the platform being played on or special qualities of the suit, I don't know, but it was all quite spectacular. I realized that their showing me these scenes was an act of kindness or a sort of gift to me personally. After all, during the writing of this book, I spent several hours a week on tennis courts.

I received these scenes in the form of real-life, three-dimensional projections. While it was felt that I was not "live" or present at these events, it was as if they were able to tap into any past happenings as if they were stored in some kind of video and replay them.

I saw their planets, their cities and the basic structure of their society. I was surprised to see thousands of planets populated. Most of them were either blue-skinned or human, but some of them were mixed. Some of the planets had been allowed to organically develop "whichever way the wind blows" and others looked and felt thoroughly planned and designed. While there were striking differences between the planets, there were similar general themes that ran through them all. This is not much different than Earth where we find differences and similarities no matter where we travel to. Everything was reflective of the 500-1000 level of energy.

Large cities are not popular in the Pleiades. Most planets had no large cities at all. Some of them had one metropolis at most. These rare gigantic cities were bright, beautiful and flawlessly designed. Imagine a futuristic utopia without the pollution, without the poverty and without the noise. Round vehicles flew silently through the air, past and above mostly white and silver buildings of creative architecture. Interestingly, buildings were not just built to house people, but each building had to have an actual function or contribution to the overall. Apart from housing people, a building might have the function of converting sun rays (or, more precisely, rays of the nearest star) into energy. Another might double as a sort of gigantic holographic screen projector for entertainment perhaps? I don't know. Yet another might be a converter of pollutants. I did not really understand the function of most buildings but I did understand that there was no building without multiple functions. With rare exceptions there were no skyscrapers. The Pleiadeans did not seem to be fans of extremely high buildings. And for the most part, there were no cities.

Pleiadeans were structured into village-like communities. Except that these villages were what we would call technologically futuristic. This is different from Earth, where the most advanced architecture, engineering and technology is applied to cities while villages are always a little "behind". Each community might have between 5,000 and 50,000 inhabitants. But, unlike on Earth, this did not mean a lack of resources. If I live in a village of 5,000 on Earth, there are a lot of things I will not have access to — the latest fashion or furniture for instance. In Pleiadean villages, access is no issue. Fashion and furniture for example, are mostly created at home. If you want a piece of furniture, you design and create one yourself. If you want new pants, you design, create and manufacture it in hour house. Pleiadean society displays maximum self-sufficiency and creativity.

As you might already expect from a people at one consciousness level higher, eating is not a priority. There are hardly any restaurants or bars. They do exist, but more for the purpose of communing and exchanging with others, than for food and drink. Much of their diet is liquid based. Some of it appears to be energy-based. The eating of fruits, vegetables and even meat is known but it appears not to be widely practiced. I saw planets in which it is not practiced at all. It is known because it was practiced in their distant past. Their bodies have evolved to process energy differently and eating non-liquid foods is viewed as outdated or even barbaric. Hence, health issues or even overweight issues are rare. If there are any health issues, they usually deal with the psychological, not the physical.

There is some conflict within and between some of the planets. Conflict per se is not a bad thing. It comes about when two different realities or energies collide. Properly resolved, a conflict is mended by ascending to a higher third way that neither of the arguing sides were occupying before. Conflict is seen as negative by

Earthlings because it is carried in an unenlightened way. For example, there was a planet among the Pleiades that its inhabitants tried to turn into a spaceship, so that it would leave its orbit and make trips to other parts of the galaxy and possibly even leave the galaxy. This might be as if California tried to break off from the U.S. and, as a whole, begin travelling the oceans and showing up near other countries. The project was controversial because it was felt that these people were overestimating their skill level.

What would have been easy for the aforementioned Creator Beings, was viewed as potentially dangerous by Pleiadeans from other planets as well as people on their home planet. They had to establish their own climate system and shield their entire globe from external radiation. The purpose of the project was also questioned. Why would the entire planet want to leave the safe and protected vicinity of the Pleiades when one could easily do so individually or in groups with interstellar devices? But for those in charge, it was about seeing whether it could be done at all. I share this anecdote to convey that Pleiadean problems are not that much different from human problems. The difference lies in scope. Even though they have more possibility than Earthlings, they still want to stretch the limits of what is possible – because they are humans. By nature, humans never rest on their laurels. The "flying planet" project was eventually deemed unsafe and shelved, but its spin off was that it became the most shielded and protected planet of the Pleiades.

The planets among the Pleiades form an Alliance. Their unity is mostly undisturbed. This is owed to their level of consciousness as well as an awareness of their similarity as compared to other extraterrestrial cultures. Similar alliances will happen on Earth. Once it is known just what kind of extraterrestrials exist out there, contrast between different cultures and ethnicities on Earth will no longer feel significant.

While there have been attempts to destroy planets and societies of the Pleiades, they are shielded by their energy level and their technology. It is not easy for the Reptilian consciousness to come close to the Pleiades; it instills fear in them. And if they do come close in spite of the energy-level contrast, their defense systems are superior to Reptilian weapons. Pleiadeans live in safety. If they face any dangers then these are from within, not from the external enemy. The Pleiadeans therefore, are less concerned with their own protection, but they protect the more vulnerable civilizations, including their ancestors on Earth. They manage to protect and save some civilizations, but not all, for the simple reason that they are not aware of all movement and activity in the galaxy and beyond. The higher your energy level, the broader your awareness and ability to act.

Having transcended the need for most foods and for hard labor, Pleiadeans involve themselves mostly in creative work, seeding planets, managing civilizations, testing different models of civilization, military protection of vulnerable societies, spiritual and higher-dimensional research and exploration and learning a number of skills.

The main difference lies in their level of consciousness, which makes their bodies lighter, their energy-selves more bright and their general mood and perception more fluid. For example, their perception of what is and isn't fun is vastly different from ours. An Earthling, for example, more easily experiences monotony and boredom. No such state or emotion exists for Pleiadeans. An analogy: Maybe you've seen a child engrossed in playing with sticks and stones for hours. There is no sense of monotony, because of the child's state of consciousness. Or perhaps you have heard a child ask an adult to do something over and over again because they think it's funny. And no matter how often you repeat the same thing, the child keeps laughing. They don't get bored because of their heightened state.

So, while Pleiadean culture, politics and economy are not that radically different from ours and you would find many things recognizable and relatable if you travelled there, the way they perceive things is radically different. There is no sense of restlessness, pressure, tediousness, heaviness, dullness. Theirs is a reality of light, laughter and amazement.

At one level higher, which is the consciousness of the beings around Sirius, interest is more deeply involved in spiritual exploration. The difference between the consciousness of Earth, Pleiades and Sirius is like the difference between a pond, a river and an ocean. Earth-Consciousness is like a pond. It is fairly stagnant. A few ripples here and there. Some activity. Perhaps some expansion. Limited depth. A pond is in an enclosed space. For there to be a radical shift to let fresh water in, some earth would have to be dug up. Pleiadean consciousness is like a river. It's always in motion, fluid, fresh, and takes in much more space than the pond. Unlike the pond, it is connected to many other bodies of water and is also connected to the ocean. Sirius-Consciousness is like that ocean. In its vastness and depth, it feeds all the waterways, seas and lakes. While there is no direct connection to the pond, there is a connection via the river that feeds the pond. The ocean harbors many more lifeforms and scenarios than a river.

It is more mysterious and contains undiscovered sea floors, hidden caves and waters deeper than anyone has explored. The best way to describe the Sirius Level of Consciousness is through feelings such as "depth", "oceanic", "deep blue", "the big blue". Both the Sirius star system and the consciousness level provide a gateway between physical reality and galactic consciousness, which is non-physical as far as we are concerned.

What does that mean, "nonphysical as far as we are concerned"? I've never really addressed this topic because it's not easy to put into Earths words or viewpoints. We discern between our "physical realm" and "non-physical realm" or the material and the spiritual. But that's only grade school thinking, in order to ascend from kindergarten thinking that "there is only the physical realm". So, the ignorant who go only by what they can see with their eyes, assume that only physical reality is real. One step higher it is felt that there is another reality. But there is no sense of discernment of this other reality. One step higher, one can discern between the spiritual realm and the astral realm. That's what I did in this book.

I went one level up in discernment because people are, by now, bored by the mere "there must be another reality". That much is already known by the majority of people.

But if we go another level of discernment higher, we arrive at the way things are viewed at the Sirius-Level. And that is, that the "Spiritual Realm" is not actually non-physical but *hyper-physical.* Or, perhaps another way to put this: Imagine a block of ice. When it melts, it becomes less dense and turns into water. When the water becomes less dense, it turns into steam. Steam, water and ice are of the same substance, manifesting in different densities. Thoughts and emotion are the steam, words and action the water and the physical result the ice. The astral realm are like rolling, forming, de-forming clouds of steam. Our physical reality is like ice.

The spiritual realm, however, is a category of its own. It's Ice that never melts, plus Water that never dirties, plus Steam that rolls around it. Or yet another way to put this: We imagine the spiritual realm to be vague and perhaps even boring. We might imagine it as a realm of light, for example. But it's not just a realm of light where we float around in bliss all day. But actually, the spiritual realm is like a grander version of the physical Universe. What a paper drawing of an apple is to a real apple, the physical universe is to the spiritual realm. The spiritual realm is not vague like steam. We have bodies in that realm. They are not our physical bodies, but something greater. Just like on Earth or the Pleiades, there are places, people, locations and activities.

Because Sirius provides an entry point to higher realms, it has been targeted by various beings who have been locked out of those realms. Their being "locked out" beings or "fallen angels" has nothing to do with injustice but is merely a consequence of their own vibration. They can re-access higher realms legitimately, by raising their own energy. Or they can try to access higher realms through cheating. I guess on Earth such activities would be called "Black Magic(k)" — the attempt to force results rather than attract them. Higher consciousness has power, lower consciousness has force. That is because, to the physical realm and those stuck there for too long, it appears as if force creates results.

Anyone who has created metal, glass or plastic or anyone who has refined oil or produced anything physical at all, knows that force and friction are a must. Some beings have come to the false belief that this attitude need be transposed to the spiritual as well as their interactions with other beings. Sirius has been one of the places where negative beings have tried to gain unwarranted entry. Most of these attempts fail. The reason they fail is because, in order to reach Sirius in consciousness or even physically, you need to elevate your consciousness. But by elevating your consciousness, your negative intentions begin to dissipate. So there are some beings who have raised their consciousness to Sirius while trying to retain or mask their negative intent. This can only be done by splitting ones personality into a type of schizophrenia, where one part is elevated and another part retains low vibrations. This is a very complicated procedure. And I realize this all must sound bizarre to you or even irrelevant to your life on Earth, but I share it because it's interesting to know just a few of the many games being played in the Universe. And I've only been talking about the Pleiades and Sirius so far, even though there are trillions of other stars I could zoom in on! Nonetheless, very few bad apples make it through the Sirus Gateway because at consciousness level 5,000 it is almost impossible to keep split off personality parts. So some negative beings have attempted another, more subtle method: They retain memory of their identity and allegiance to a lower-density group. Let's say you are of the Serpent group of beings (and I keep using them as an example, because they are the ones humans are at least vaguely familiar with, even though there is no shortage of other groups belonging to more dense realms). You swear an oath of allegiance to your group and its agenda *forever.* Then you ascend, with the intention of retaining your identity and allegiance.

Once you pass the gate, your soul-level programming is meant to reactivate. Then, with your new-found powers, you work to subvert the spiritual realm (or, in this case, the galactic realm, which is a lower part of the overall spiritual realm) on behalf of your reptilian buddies below. And while this has been attempted and sometimes even achieved partially, it is not only difficult and unlikely but ultimately ineffective. Let's transpose this method to earthly realms: Let's say you're a Chinese intelligence operative seeking to infiltrate the CIA. And let's say you are groomed early on to become a double agent. You are sent from China to a U.S. school. You grow up in the U.S. Then you enter a university of which your handlers know the CIA recruits from. You study the subjects of interest to the CIA. And then the day comes that they recruit you. You finally made it.

But it's not that simple. The problem is, that by the time you made it, you have already become "contaminated" by U.S. society. It has formed your mentality and relationships. In order to "make it" you will have had to get "contaminated" by it. Your original sponsors no longer know if they can trust you. Not to mention that leadership back "home", which you don't even feel as home anymore, may have changed and no longer be pursuing their agenda. Moreover, you are only one person, whereas your American CIA colleagues are many. Finally, due to your Chinese origin, someone will be keeping a watchful eye over you.

Similar has applied to imposters trying to cheat their way through the Sirius Gateway. By the time they reach that level, they lose interest in cheating. Or they come clean. Or they see how wonderful it is up there and never want to return again. Some forget their mission altogether. Some switch sides. And in the extremely rare cases that negative infiltration is achieved, there are plenty of higher authorities in the Universe that can easily detect and erase the issue.

So negative beings came up with yet another variation to cheat their way upwards (and that's the nature of negative beings — they believe they have to force and cheat in order to accomplish anything). They attempt to brainwash their subjects at a soul level. Having discovered that mere mental brainwashing does not hold up and in fact begins falling apart at levels 500, attempts are made to manipulate the soul. As I write this, I'm amused at the hilarity of their futile attempts. The soul cannot be manipulated, in the way they want, but they don't know that. Consciousness ascension implies a purification of the soul and there is simply no real entry if one does not represent higher vibration. And in the rare cases there is, one is found out quickly. Similarly, I recall someone once trying to attend one of my seminars for free. There were forty people in attendance, and this particular person looked completely out of place. He was spotted so easily. It turned out that he hadn't paid entry and was asked to leave. Games of subversion and spying may be doable on Earth, but they are hardly doable at Sirius.

It being a gateway, many of the beings that live on planets around Sirius are at the "leading edge" of physical civilization. Sirius is not the only galactic gateway to higher realms, but it is the only one in our direct vicinity. There could be a dozen others throughout the galaxy, maybe more. It is the first area one arrives to when descending and the last area one experiences before ascending. Many spiritual teachers on Earth have mistaken this state of consciousness with "enlightenment". Specifically, Buddhist and Hindu teachers have talked of this realm with reverence. They speak of a deep peace that overcame them, a no-mind state, a void, a vastness, an awareness of unspeakable secrets, an initiation into the mysteries of the Universe, cosmic consciousness, etc. But as high as it is compared to us, it's still not the full spiritual realm. Their oceanic consciousness is reflected in that their planets have many actual oceans. Their buildings are what we would consider gigantic. Imagine standing on a platform, looking out into a vast and wild ocean, that descends into a bottomless waterfall before it reaches the platform. The platform itself is attached to a structure that is so big, that if I were to see the entire structure, I would not see you because your body is too small compared to it. I wouldn't even see the railing of the platform. Beside the building you are smaller than an ant. From an earthly perspective, there is not all that much physical activity occurring because the beings there live mostly within. They are semi-physical and their explorations are in consciousness. So there might be one building the size of New York, surrounded by ocean and that would make up the entire planet. That is, the whole planet is covered by ocean and one gigantic structure is built on it and perhaps one beacon like structure for travelers elsewhere. "Not much going on here," an Earthling would say. You'd travel by ship for months and would see only ocean and perhaps the occasional dolphin, whale or creatures unknown to Earth. Then, in the distance, this vast block or tower would appear. Many buildings there are beige or light brown, similar to colors found in the Middle East. On some parts there might be stretches of window, reflecting the blue of the water, but a building could also go on for miles without balconies, platforms or windows. And that's it.

I've just described an entire planet around Sirius. It is not about what is happening in the external, physical worlds there. The physical parts are only made in order for new arrivals or level-descenders to ease into the physical or for those soon to ascend to ease out of it. Any Earthling put to one of those planets in Earth Consciousness, would feel lost and lonely. They'd ask, "What is there to DO here?" Meanwhile, those of Sirius are more into BEING. They spend a lot of time outside of their bodies, traversing the gate to higher realms, visiting the astral realms, fulfilling astral-support duties, assisting planet seeders and civilization builders, learning themselves about planet creation and management or even travelling to other galaxies. At one level higher, the understanding of one's own galaxy and others is quite comprehensive, similar to a more advanced Earthling having a clearer idea of this worlds various countries, languages and customs.

The beings of Sirius do not have that comprehensive understanding of galaxies. Their travels are pinpointed to specific locations and work or assistance being done there, similar to an Earthling just travelling to one village in Kenya, without a full grasp of Africa as a whole. To such a person, "Africa" is one idea and "pretty much the same" all over the continent. Anyone who says "like the starving African children" is at such a base awareness level that there is no discernment of the vast differences in Africa. Most Africans are not actually starving, unless you have only heard about Africa in the propagandistic media of Earth. Just travel there and you quickly realize that hardly anyone is starving. Bustling cities and economic trade abound. Similarly, a Sirian might travel to another galaxy and be aware of only one star system there and come to conclusions about the entire galaxy based on that one system. The beings of Sirius normally do not use spaceships and interstellar devices or stargates to travel. These things are left to the denser beings of the Pleiades. They travel in consciousness. And again, this experience is not vaguer and more non-physical, that's only the human perspective. It is hyper-physical.

As you pass the gateway to the galactic realm, you enter an area that I have already described in some detail in my book, *Lives of the Soul.* The Galactic Authority exist as spiritual or hyper-physical beings. We are now at the lowest level of the spiritual realm. Many that exist on this realm have had a previous physical existence and many haven't. You can tell the difference in that those that have never been physical have a certain purity and innocence about them, whereas former physical-universe beings have something stronger and more complete about them.

That is in fact the purpose of descending into the physical in order to eventually ascend back to the hyper-physical: A training program to gain radiance, competence, understanding and strength. And again, it's not unlike Earth: Put a girl who has been protected and pampered in a rich families house all her life and never travelled, beside a hardened war veteran and you'll feel, see and hear the difference easily. There is something pure about the girl and something mature about the veteran. Both pure souls and mature souls are required for the management of a galaxy. I call these two types of souls incarnates and non-incarnates. The non-incarnates have a healing effect on the whole. The incarnates have experience. The non-incarnates are a source of joy. The incarnates are revered.

It takes a lot of courage to incarnate to physical levels. Some get lost in the physical for thousands of years.

Some get lost for millions of years — the Reptilians are a great example of having gotten lost. They are lost to a point they don't even understand the spiritual realm. To find an Earth analogy: Let's say you get kicked out from your home and go travel on your own. And you never return back home. Eventually, you'll forget all about where you came from. All you remember is getting kicked out, so going back is not appealing to you in any case. That summarizes the Reptilian situation. Some of the Reptilian race, however, realize there must be something more than their arid worlds, wars and enslavement of entire star systems and they begin ascending again. All of reality can be seen on a spectrum of ascent, descent and traverse. And that's what the Christian cross is supposed to symbolize in my opinion. There are three paths, up or down (vertical) or across (horizontal). The Christian cross has its vertical line at the upper part of the vertical line to indicate that "if you are going to traverse the realms, instead of ascend or descend, let it at least be one of the higher realms. If you are wondering why you have never heard of this before, it's because it comes from my unique viewpoint and knowledge. The things I communicate are not derivative, but partially sourced from other realms.

Above the Galactic Authority, we find the Authority of the Universe. And you might assume that this is the ultimate, highest, greatest Authority there is, what we call God, but it isn't. There is yet another Authority above that, which manages the Multiverse, which is a collection of countless universes. And then there is another authority above that, which oversees the Omniverse. That is, as far as I can tell, the Highest Authority, as far as we are concerned. But at our level of consciousness, it doesn't really matter whether you focus on the Authority of the whole Universe, that of the Multiverse or that of the Omniverse, because all have trillions of energy levels far beyond anything you'll ever need. The Galactic Authority is able to create and form planets, bodies and physical matter. The Universal Authority is able to create infinite souls themselves. The Multiverse Authority must stay undefined in this book for the simple reason that I don't grasp it. However, for a basic definition of these realms, see my video, "The Nature of Infinity".

There is so much to learn about the galaxy and the Universe, that we are not yet at a stage where we'd penetrate the Multiverse, not to mention the Omniverse. Your individual soul is created from the level of the Multiverse. Consciousness itself or energy itself, or life itself is created from the Omniverse level. From this paragraph you can appreciate how ridiculously limited our earthly "knowledge" is. Yet, on the other hand, "as above so below". By the way Earth works, you can somewhat glean how higher contexts work. As explained in the aforementioned video presentation, each larger context contains all smaller contexts within it. Existence then, is shaped like an onion and, when symbolically displayed, you best use several concentric circles. In my 2010 book, I mentioned an old science fiction book called, *Star Maker*, written in 1937 by Olaf Stapledon. That book, in my view, is not actually science fiction. It describes the nature of things quite well. Just like me, the author must have seen these things while travelling out of body. Suspiciously, the book as now published on the market, has been rewritten in various sections by the publisher in order to "make it easier to digest". The version of the book as it is now sold and the original are different and no longer convey the same level of enlightenment. We are all familiar with religious books being rewritten and falsified, but who would have thought the same is done with sci-fi?. So no, this is not a book recommendation. Instead of relying on me or other authors, I recommend you learn to see for yourself.

CHAPTER SEVEN

HOW TO TRAVEL THE UNIVERSE

I'd like to give you clear instructions on how to travel the Universe if you do not happen to own a spaceship or a teleportation device (also known as a stargate). I know that this kind of arcane information is lacking on Earth. All these books out there make grandiose claims but do very little to help people experience any of it. So at the end of the day, reading up on all of that is like reading a 10-million-page menu without getting anything to eat.

The good news is, that you already travel the Universe every single night. Or what did you think your soul is doing all night while body and mind are asleep? Did you really think your essence just lies there in the bedroom all night? Of course not. Your soul undertakes its nightly journeys out of body. Some of these journeys are remembered as "dreams". Most of your dreams are travels to the astral realm. As explained earlier, you have an astral double that you can operate so that you can see these realms. But frankly, the astral realm, that is easily accessible through drugs and your double, should not be your main target. These are lower-level places. They might suffice for beginners, but your ultimate aim should be the spiritual realms.

The Universe as you know it, actually exists at varying levels of consciousness. The Pleiades for example, while obviously physical, vibrate at a higher level than Earth. Sirius vibrates one level higher still. By becoming a vibratory frequency that vibrates both higher than Pleiades and Sirius — Galactic Consciousness so to speak — it becomes fairly easy to visit either Sirius, the Pleiades or trillions of other places below Galactic Consciousness. If you want access and entry to certain realms to be easy, you have to be coming from a higher context than those realms.

So the challenge of out-of-body travel is not with "achieving it" — you travel outside of your body already, anyway and every night! There are countless books out there that make it seem as if "astral projection" (a limiting misnomer) or the "out-of-body experience" would require some training and effort and its achievement would be magical. There is nothing magical about it. It's as natural and normal as walking. Or perhaps only slightly more difficult than walking, as with walking you have four directions: forward, backward, left and right.

With out of body travel you have two additional directions: forward, backward, left, right, down and up.

It is for this reason that I have enjoyed flying lessons in a small plane, as well as paragliding lessons. These make it easier to familiarize oneself with the up and down options. In fact, these two additional dimensions of movement are corresponding indicators of our next higher level of consciousness. At one level higher still, you will be able to travel forward, backward, left, right, up, down and through time. And at one level higher yet, you will get to know a dimension that cannot be put into human words.

The challenge, then, is in remembering your out-of-body journeys, as well as consciously choosing where you would like to travel. Well, you do consciously choose it already, but it is not your conscious mind but rather your conscious soul or your astral-self (double) doing the choosing while the mind is sleeping. You would probably like your conscious mind to target a few destinations of interest. And if your astral-self is doing the choosing, it is well and good to get your conscious mind involved, so that you do not always have to travel to those *confusing realms of weirdness.*

Another important distinction to make, is that dreaming and out-of-body travel are essentially the same thing. You are travelling out-of-body every night and whatever you perceive during those travels, is what you are experiencing while no longer connected to the body. Sometimes you perceive the phantasmagoria of the astral realm, which interacts with garbled nonsense of your subconscious. Such dreams are like garbage processing and have no real value. Sometimes you dream at a higher realm and experience great clarity and joy. Sometimes you travel to places on Earth. Sometimes you time travel. Sometimes you visit parallel timelines. Someday humans will have enough clarity to write an elaborate classification system of realms. In fact, I believe that some of the books in aforementioned "secret library" were describing various other realms in which other laws and mentalities exist. In fact, by the "feel" I got from the books, many were describing the endless layers and worlds of the astral realm. The astral realm, while limited in energetic vibration, seems almost unlimited in creative variation. The beings there are imbued with creativity, just like you, and spend millennia crafting various worlds to experience. There are countless books on Earth that describe specific "countries" of the astral realm. "Alice in Wonderland" by Lewis Carroll is one such example. You will find a lot of philosophers and occultists take the astral realm very seriously, but it's not all that important nor all that pleasant. Imagine an amusement park full of weird rides, noise, circuses, freakshows, harlequins, masked parties, alcohol, drugs, psychedelic rides and whatnot. That's what the astral realm feels like. It's fascinating at first, but once you have seen it as often as I have, it grows boring and even annoying.

—

The first step to travelling the Universe is to sharpen your dream recall. If you really want to travel this path, it is time to acknowledge that there is a whole other world out there that another side of you sees every night and you have to want in on the action. As your dream recall improves, your awareness and understanding of this other world improves. You will have to stop thinking of your dreams as vague and meaningless images. Treat your dreams as actual trips you took. And how to sharpen dream recall? By repeating your dreams every morning. You either run them through your mind again, right after waking up. Or you tell them to your partner if one such is waking up beside you. Or you write them down. The longer you do this, the more dreams you remember. As you become more aware of your dreams, you soon become more aware within your dreams, and that is what allows your conscious mind to participate in night travels choices.

And what if you do not remember any of your dreams? Well, then you are about as far away from the other side as can be. It means you primarily exist as a mind of daily life, with little awareness of anything else. In that case I recommend you gain a deeper interest in your dreams. Read up on dreams. Read up on lucid dreaming. Try out programs on lucid dreaming. Read my previous materials on lucid dreaming (as described in my book *Being Higher Self*). Turn off your Wi-Fi and mobile data at night, as their repetitive frequencies can obstruct full night time awareness (I am not saying that these frequencies are harmful, but rather that their sameness obstructs your ability to *change* your frequency). Attempt focused visualization while falling asleep.

The trick to out-of-body travel is staying awake while falling asleep. Not an easy task and completely contradictory. If you can get your body to relax so deeply that it falls asleep, while a small part of your conscious mind stays awake, you will witness your energy-body (soul) leaving the physical body.

Apart from intensified dream recall, deep and thorough relaxation while staying aware, is the second key to travelling the Universe. Deep relaxation can be practiced with meditation, mantras, prayers, deep massages, specially crafted sounds, breathing techniques, attention exercises and many other methods described in previous books.

Navigation in the astral and spiritual realms is not through linear time but through attention. To give you an example of this: Let's say in daily life, you have breakfast with your spouse at 8 o'clock, then you drive to work and then you see your colleagues. Events appear as a linear progression through time. Both the astral realm and the high spiritual realms, do not have this progression (semi-physical consciousness levels such as those of the beings of the Pleiades and Sirius still have a sense of time, albeit more expanded). So if you were to put your attention on breakfast with your spouse, that's where you would be. If you then put attention on driving to work, that's what would happen. But if you then intentionally or inadvertently remember breakfast with your spouse, you'd suddenly be back there again. And then attention might go to your work at the office and you'd be there. From this you can see why it's important to practice attention control. What you think of, there you are, especially in the astral realm. One could say that the lower astral realm is a "hell of one's own making". If you die with negative feelings and thoughts, you will resonate with others on your level and gravitate toward already existing negative worlds and add your negativity to it. On the spiritual realms your thoughts and attention also have an influence, but fortunately there are greater influences that maintain positive scenarios even if you don't. These realms are so overwhelmingly positive that it's almost impossible to think anything less than them.

In reports of near-death-experiences, many people say that they enter a dark tunnel at the end of which there is a light. This is actually the universal procedure of being born into another realm. It begins as a dark tunnel and ends into the light. The same perception is present when we are born into this life. At a very low level of consciousness, the amount of light you are born into "on the other side" is not that bright. Having lived a negative life, you might get stuck in the lower astral realm. This is what religions meant when they said "hell". However, your stay in those realms is not a "punishment" but merely the law of attraction in action. You are there by your own choice and not "eternally damned". The idea of "eternal damnation in hell" is one of the most idiotic concepts to have ever been sold to humans as "religion".

As the lower astral and higher spiritual realms are timeless, the concept of "eternal" doesn't apply in the same way it would to us timebound Earthlings. The religious concepts of "eternal life in Heaven" and "eternal suffering in Hell" mean that both "Heaven" and "Hell" exist outside of time as we know it. Timelessness in that sense, is indeed "eternal". But to think that after one trillion years of suffering you still need to suffer some more and then after ten trillion years of punishment, you need to be punished some more, is not a religious or spiritual concept but a sadistic misinterpretation. Likewise, the idea of "eternal bliss" when you "reach a state of enlightenment" or "go to Heaven" is just as nonsensical. It's not that you live in the same state for a trillion years and then another ten trillion years and another few million years, and then for another quadrillion eons. You still experience purpose, challenge, adventure, discovery, learning and growth even in "Heaven". The idea of sitting on a cloud and playing a harp for eternity is off the mark.

Let's revisit this image shown earlier. The astral realm is a fairly tiny band of foggy energy around and inside the Earth. Strictly speaking, lower-astral is inside the Earth, mid-astral on Earth and higher-astral around Earth and in the solar system. So there is really not that much merit in travelling the astral realm. You'll want to at least go extraterrestrial, which would, for example be the consciousness-level of the Pleiades. In fact, the word "extraterrestrial" is a misnomer here. You'll want to go extrasolar and transcend the solar system altogether.

Make no mistake: The Pleiades are not the only place or system at this higher level. I am merely using them as a typical example of a particular consciousness level because they are related to humanity. The same applies to the semi-physical Sirius level of consciousness. There are numerous other portals, stars and realms that are on that level, but Sirius serves as an example. Galactic Consciousness is one level above that and the same level could be achieved by a consciousness of other galaxies than The Milky Way. In fact, people who are merely interested in the nature of galaxies, are actually at an above average consciousness level already.

Above that is "The Field" which is not merely some vague energy, but actually includes entire cities and countries. It is what the religions call "Heaven". However, there is not just "one" Heaven, there are many levels (as described in my book, *Journeys in Spectral Consciousness*). From everything you have read about

"The Field", you probably think it's all non-physical. But there are actually areas of "Heaven" that are made of what I would call "hyper-physical" lands. Allow me to explain: Beings who have lived for some time in the physical realm, have come to enjoy and like aspects of it. Therefore, hyper-physical realms were created way up in the spiritual spheres. You do not have to forever float around as a ball of energy, you can have a body and specific places and objects. What makes the hyper-physical plane different is that there is no suffering and everything is trillions of times more beautiful.

If you haven't guessed it yourself yet: The image above represents "The Way Home" for most human souls. In my view, it is what ancients referred to as "The Tree of Life". A state of enlightenment at death will result in you passing through all portals, directly to the highest levels. Any state less than that and you'll end up somewhere along the way. But "Galactic Consciousness" is not so bad. It's vastly more exciting than mere Earth Consciousness.

The higher your consciousness level, the brighter the light you see when you are reborn on the other side after you die on Earth. At an even higher level, you not only see light, you also here the "music of the spheres". And at an even higher level, the main event lies in what you are feeling. Death, ego and time are intricately linked. Without one, there cannot be another. It is the ego that exists within time and at the end of its time, there is death. It is the ego that is worried about time and death. For the soul, there is no time; and if there is no time, there is no end; and if there is no end, there is no death.

Once you learn dream recall and by extension lucid dreaming, as well as staying awake while falling asleep and by extension out-of-body travel, you can then proceed to learn how to target specific locations and also which locations are worth targeting. One of the reasons this book was written is so that you know that the Pleiades are worth targeting as a potential travel destination and that planets such as, say, Saturn, are not worth targeting as our solar system is mostly astral-realm material. I've already taught how to target places in this chapter but I'll spell it out for you in case you missed it: By focusing attention. So you might take an image of the Pleiades and look at it for a while before falling asleep, memorizing it so that you can visualize it with your eyes closed:

In order to be transported there either in your dreams or out of body travels, all you have to do is intend and focus. It has to be clear which specific area you mean. It won't do to focus on just any star because that will result in you ending up in just any star system. You see, for lower consciousness "it all looks the same". But for refined awareness, it's not all the same. Different stars and star systems have different qualities. And not many stars in our Milky Way have the level and quality of the Pleiades. You do not have to worry about an overly exact visualization, it just has to be clear that you are referring to the Pleiades. So, you should get a good enough impression of them to at least resemble the system as seen from Earth. Unless you are a strong focuser, you don't even have to maintain visualization of seven stars at the same time. You can instead see the vague overall cluster. As always in visualization, what you intend and feel is more important than what exactly you are seeing. Seeing is merely used to pinpoint location and generate feeling. Beginners should focus on the general overall vicinity of the Pleiades. If you are more advanced, you can pick specific stars or even planets (or even cities, neighborhoods, houses).

So how long do you focus on your destination? That again, depends on your expertise. The seasoned traveler will only need one brief intention, lasting two seconds, to end up in the Pleiades. The beginner ought to focus without continually until the body is asleep. While the body falls asleep, the energy body will begin vibrating and detach from you and you will instantly be transported to your destination.

Travel in consciousness has a few advantages and disadvantages toward physical travel in spaceships or stargates (yes, the teleportation portals shown in the TV sci-fi series "Stargate" are real and they do exist on Earth. Just because you happen not to know about it doesn't mean it's not real).

Advantages: Its quicker. You are more flexible. There are no health risks for the physical body. You are not bound by too many regulations. You can meet whoever you choose (Stargates are guarded and you'd have to deal with their equivalent of immigration officers). It costs nothing (do you have a trillion to spare on a lightspeed spaceship?).

The disadvantage is that the environment, perception and communication may not be quite as stable as in the physical Universe. Memory of the event will be vaguer, unless you bring everything to paper right after the visit (like I did with this book). But there are really small concessions to make compared to the advantages.

To summarize the three abilities required to travel the Universe:

1. Improved awareness of other realms (through dream recall)

2. Ability to consciously leave your body (by staying awake while falling asleep)

3. Ability to intend and focus (by visualizing specific locations)

If not easy, the task is at least simple.

What makes this kind of practice moderately important is the fact that the consciousness of humanity is clouded and some practice is required to break the fog. Most of what is *actually* going on is invisible to your eyes. Through being only involved in what you see around you with your eyes, you are missing out on 99% of what is happening.

If you would like your travels to go beyond the mere astral band of muddy energy, the only thing you really need to develop strongly is a sense of love. Love equals higher consciousness. I recommend my freely available video "Love is Stronger than Mind" on this.

From the few descriptions given in this chapter, you should be able to travel the Universe. I could write an entire manual on out-of-body travel or lucid dreaming. In fact, I have written entire books on that such as my German language book, *Astralreisen*, exclusively for out-of-body travel, or my German language book, *Zeitreisen*, for time travel or my English language book, *Being Higher Self*, which contains a long chapter on lucid dreaming. However, the higher your consciousness level, the less description you need and the more self-discipline you should have. Above a certain level of consciousness, you no longer have to be spoon fed step-by-step procedures, just like a child of more mature age needn't be taught every little detail of living. For example, when I say "practice focusing while falling asleep" or "stay awake while falling asleep" it should be clear to you that there are hundreds of ways of focusing and that you can choose your preferred way. You could focus on a candle flame or on a thought or on the Pleiades. Or you could have a little bit of coffee to stay mentally alert. Or you could practice setting a timer beep, that keeps you somewhat awake. In fact, I have described these things in great detail in countless books and videos, providing more information than you will ever need to go on these journeys. It is not knowledge or know-how that you lack.

If anything, most people lack energy and self-discipline. At a mid-level of consciousness, a person might be living a life where he doesn't have the energy to practice at night time. All he wants, after a "hard day at work" is to fall asleep and lose himself. The idea of travelling planets, stars and galaxies seems distant and unrealistic.

Whatever skill you would like to learn, requires making time and investing attention. In this sense, travelling the Universe is no different than playing the piano. If you want to play the piano, you don't just take one lesson, you practice it until you are good at it.

In some cases, however, you'll have a protective field around you that does not allow you to travel. I don't know how many people are protected from seeing other realms, but in these cases, even practice does not help. Whether you are one of the protected and therefore ineligible for out-of-body travel, you will see after about one to two weeks of nightly practice. If you have the permission and ability to do it, you will gain quick results. If you do not gain quick results, then it is not for you and your energy might be better invested with other things. Of course, even then it's not impossible for you to achieve, but it would take a little more soul-searching, fear-releasing and practicing.

I cannot confirm that out-of-body travel is dangerous. Love is a protective shield against all threat. The only thing dangerous is your own fear because it makes you vulnerable.

Yes, there are all sorts of entities and strange energies flying around out there, but in general, negative entities are afraid of humans. Why do you think they try to scare humans? You only try to scare someone you are afraid of. Being afraid and scaring others go together. If they manage to scare you, then they have managed to get some control of you, then they can penetrate your space. So, the very best thing you can do, is to practice calm and kindness throughout the day — this attitude will transfer to your night travels.

When I was a teenager, I used to take walks in the woods at night. Knowing that woods at night are teeming with all sorts of non-physical entities — this is one of their territories — I practiced staying calm and centered while surrounded by them. That prepared me well for out-of-body travels. I wouldn't recommend you do that, unless you are very strong inside. And I wouldn't recommend you out-of-body travel if you aren't confident inside. Being worried and fearful will get you in trouble with both humans and non-physical beings. There are two emotions that neutralize fear: love and hate. Some beings choose the path of hate to overcome fear. Some choose the path of love. As long as you have love in your heart, no harm will come to you. Hate, on the other hand, extinguishes fear but it also densifies your energy to a point where you are cut off from higher realms altogether.

So the ultimate message here is to “choose Love”. And as generic, vague and overused that sounds, it will take you upwards.

ABOUT THE AUTHOR

Frederick E. Dodson, born in the USA 1974 currently lives in Arizona. He loves viewing life from many different viewpoints and putting spiritual knowledge into the practice of everyday life rather than following the 9-to-5 routine of a "steady job". In his twenties he wrote and published 15 books and held many hundreds of workshops, talks and seminars on the topic of reality creation. Lately however, he has retreated from teaching somewhat and only conducts one course a year. He has started viewing "experiencing joy" higher than "teaching others". Why? Because everyone has their own version of the truth and the purpose of his life is not to get others to agree with him, but to have fun. His favourite activities in the meantime include scuba diving, surfing the internet, writing, collecting movies, travelling and lucid dreaming.

If you liked this book and want to learn more, check out my website at www.realitycreation.org.

Printed in Dunstable, United Kingdom

70785070R00224